THE
CATASTROPHIC
WORRIER

Why You Worry & How to Stop

GRAHAM DAVEY, PhD

New Harbinger Publications, Inc.

NEW HARBINGER PUBLICATIONS is a registered trademark of New Harbinger Publications, Inc.

New Harbinger Publications is an employee-owned company.

Copyright © 2023 by Graham Davey
New Harbinger Publications, Inc.
5674 Shattuck Avenue
Oakland, CA 94609
www.newharbinger.com

Cover design by Sara Christian

Acquired by Jennye Garibaldi

Edited by Gretel Hakanson

Library of Congress Cataloging-in-Publication Data

Names: Davey, Graham, author.
Title: The catastrophic worrier : why you worry & how to stop / by Graham Davey.
Description: Oakland, CA : New Harbinger Publications, [2023] | Includes bibliographical references.
Identifiers: LCCN 2022032705 | ISBN 9781648480348 (trade paperback)
Subjects: LCSH: Worry. | Anxiety. | BISAC: SELF-HELP / Anxieties & Phobias | SELF-HELP / Self-Management / Stress Management
Classification: LCC BF575.W8 D38 2023 | DDC 152.4/6--dc23/eng/20220914
LC record available at https://lccn.loc.gov/2022032705

Printed in the United States of America

25   24   23

10   9   8   7   6   5   4   3   2   1   First Printing

"Under normal circumstances, worrying is adaptive and motivates us to plan for the future. But for many of us, it can spiral out of control such that we worry incessantly and intensely about even small issues. One word for this process is 'catastrophizing,' and Graham Davey is widely acknowledged as a world expert on this topic. In this well-written, easy-to-read manual, you will learn about the origins and nature of catastrophic worry, and more importantly, you'll learn the latest evidence-based strategies for bringing this out-of-control process back under your control."

—**David H. Barlow, PhD**, professor emeritus of psychology and psychiatry at Boston University, founder of the Center for Anxiety & Related Disorders, and author of more than ninety books and clinical manuals on anxiety and emotional disorders

"As far as we know, humans are the only species that can anticipate the future and be anxious about what might happen in that future. Worry is commonly focused on things that never happen, and is a cause for considerable distress and ill health. In these times of uncertainty and coming out of COVID lockdowns, 'worry' amongst many of us has increased. It is therefore timely that Graham Davey, a leading psychologist in this area, guides us expertly and gently through the origins and bases of worry, and how we can work on ourselves to minimize its impact. This will be immensely helpful for those who find their minds spiraling off into all kinds of worries."

—**Paul Gilbert, PhD, FBPsS, OBE**, professor of clinical psychology at the university of Derby, and visiting professor at the university of Queensland; president of The Compassionate Mind Foundation; and author of *The Compassionate Mind*

"Are you a worrywart? Are you consumed by worries about your future, your health, and even minor matters? Then you might be dealing with catastrophic worrying. Graham Davey's book will gently guide you through the process of overcoming catastrophic worrying. Written by one of the foremost experts on this topic, this book will help you stop the worry machine and get your life back."

—**Stefan G. Hofmann, PhD**, Alexander von Humboldt professor, and author of *CBT for Social Anxiety*

"Davey has spent thirty years conducting innovative research on worry and anxiety. In this unique book, he draws on his own exacting studies and that of other key researchers in considering why we worry, what makes us vulnerable to excessive worrying, and what to do about it. This is a valuable resource for professionals in the field, and sufferers seeking a deeper understanding and associated exercises to transform catastrophic worry into 'smart worry.'"

> —**Adrian Wells, PhD**, professor of clinical and experimental psychopathology at The University of Manchester, UK; and director of the Anxiety, Depression and Psychological Therapies Research Unit at Greater Manchester Mental Health NHS Trust

"Graham Davey summarizes decades of research on worry and anxiety into a practical, accessible, and engaging book that explains why we worry, why we *keep* worrying, and importantly, how we can reduce our worrying. Readers are guided through evidence-supported strategies and exercises that work, and that will help them to live more fulfilling lives. A must-read for all talented worriers."

> —**Peter McEvoy**, professor of clinical psychology at Curtin University, senior clinical psychologist at the Centre for Clinical Interventions, and associate editor of the *Journal of Anxiety Disorders*

"*The Catastrophic Worrier* is a delightfully accessible book, written by an internationally recognized expert who has researched worry for many years. Topics include the causes of worry, and practical steps the reader can take to become a more adaptive worrier. Addressed to readers who are burdened by worry that has become uncontrollable and distressing, it will also interest psychology students, mental health professionals, and anyone interested in how the mind works."

> —**Richard Bentall**, professor of clinical psychology at the University of Sheffield, fellow of the British Academy, and author of *Madness Explained*

For my mother, Betty, and my daughters, Kate and Lizzie.

Contents

Introduction

Worrying is one of the most common human activities—yet studies claim that 90 percent of what we worry about never actually happens. So why do we do it?

Worry signals that there's something threatening or challenging on the horizon, and we need to deal with it. But do we resolve these problems in our head? Usually far from it. For many of us, worrying rarely offers the comforting solutions to our problems that we're looking for. Instead, it simply becomes a search for even more problems that we believe might be hidden in the situation we're worrying about. This is known as catastrophic worrying and is the central topic of this book.

Catastrophic worrying can be characterized by that repeated "What if...?" question you ask yourself. You resolutely begin worrying by trying to find a solution that'll resolve your worry, but you end up in a mess after having made the worry seem significantly worse than it was at the start, and you feel considerably more anxious and distressed than when you originally identified the problem. To add to this, everything seems completely out of your control—you can't stop worrying, the catastrophic outcomes of your worry seem ever more likely to happen the more you think about them, and your worry's grown from a molehill into a mountain.

Uncontrolled catastrophic worrying affects your mental health and your physical health. It interferes with your daily living, your work performance, your family life, and your relationships. It keeps you awake at night and distracts you during the day. So, I'll ask you again: Why do you do it?

At this point, you might want to interrupt and tell me you're a "born worrier." However, in this book, I'll argue that the born worrier is a myth. You *become* a worrier, and if you've learned to be a worrier, then you can also unlearn that tendency.

In this book, I'll describe more than thirty years of research that has helped us understand why we worry, the developmental processes that turn us into worriers, and why worrying so regularly goes wrong and turns into a compulsive, distressing, and uncontrollable activity. But we do have solutions for chronic worrying, and throughout the book, I also describe simple exercises you can use to assess your own worrying, manage some "bad" worry habits, and finally develop some skills that will turn you into a "smart" worrier who can solve problems and implement solutions. (Additional materials are available for download at the website for this book at http://www.newharbinger.com/50348.) You can then say good-bye to being a lifelong slave to the distress and confusion that is catastrophic worrying.

—Graham Davey
February 2022

PART I

WHAT IS WORRYING, AND WHERE DOES IT COME FROM?

CHAPTER 1

Making Mountains Out of Molehills

The Process of Catastrophic Worrying

Roadmap of the chapter. This chapter introduces you to catastrophic worrying—a very common form of worrying in which thinking about the worry just seems to make it worse. Ever had that experience? Most of us have. In this chapter, I'll describe the various psychological processes that contribute to catastrophic worrying that make it relentless and distressing. You'll have the opportunity to see if you recognize yourself in any of these examples, and at the end of the chapter, you can try an exercise that will measure your tendency to catastrophize.

Let's begin with a serious piece of overthinking.

"For a long time, I believed that my disaster-focused way of thinking was normal. I thought there was nothing unusual about the fact that something mildly unfortunate would happen to me, and in a matter of seconds, my brain would invent a chain of terrible outcomes that I convinced myself were almost certain to happen in the near future. Sometimes, the catalyst didn't even have to be mildly unfortunate—it could be perfectly ordinary. I could get an email from my boss asking to hop on a quick call, which is a situation that happens to people all over the world every single day. But within seconds, my brain would take this to mean that I must have made a huge mistake on one of my assignments without realizing it, that the whole company was in jeopardy of collapsing, and that I would, of course, be fired, then lose my health insurance, have no income, and would be forced to live in my parents' basement."[1]

The human brain is a very sophisticated piece of biological machinery—so sophisticated, in fact, that in a matter of seconds, it can take someone from hearing the "ping" of an email arriving in their inbox to developing a vivid image of abject misery as they live out the rest of their life in their parents' dingy basement many hundreds of miles away. And all the steps required to make this thought transition from a simple, common daily event to lifelong poverty and banishment seem to be entirely out of your control. If you're a catastrophic worrier, it's your brain doing all this, but it's like a badly trained dog racing away from you in the park, oblivious to your shouts to come back and behave. You simply can't stop overthinking.

Simple everyday things in life can erupt dramatically into mountain peaks of distress. There's a small stain on the carpet. Will you be late for work if the clocks in the house aren't accurate? There's a slight scratch on the car—you need to look very closely to see it—but you know it's there.

Have you had these kinds of thoughts about simple, everyday things? Have they bugged you all day, entering your head uncontrollably and bullying you into making them the focus of your attention? Then do these "bullying" thoughts drive you to start asking "What if…?" questions: What if I can't get that stain out of the carpet? What if the clocks are wrong? What if everyone else can see that scratch on the car?

This is the most common form of pathological worrying and is known as "catastrophizing." Catastrophizing is a form of worrying where you simply go from one bad thought to another and end up exaggerating the problem. If you experience catastrophic worrying, you know that it's not just simply a form of thinking that only races from one bad happening to another; it also causes you distress and seems to be entirely uncontrollable. It's so uncontrollable, in fact, that you probably start to believe that this is the way your brain is wired, and there's absolutely nothing you can do about it.

This is why many chronic worriers often say, "I'm a born worrier"— because they've come to the conclusion that their way of thinking about things can't be changed so they must have been born that way.[2] If this has come as a bit of a shock to you, I'll explain the origins of catastrophic worrying in more detail in chapter 2. But the important message here is that if you're a catastrophic worrier, then you've learned to think in "What if…?" ways—so much so that your brain now performs this act of catastrophizing automatically and effortlessly. But the positive in all this is that if a behavior like catastrophizing is learned, it can also be unlearned.

Like many people, I'm also a worrier—but now it afflicts me only occasionally. Some of the worst hours of my life have been spent lying awake in bed worrying in the early hours of the morning—a prime time for catastrophic worrying. Something that seems perfectly ordinary about tomorrow will pop into my head. *I've got to drive to the station tomorrow, but what if I can't park the car? Will I miss my train? What will I do about that important appointment? I won't even be able to call to say I'm late if my phone's dead!* I'll be tirelessly thinking through potential scenarios and mentally rehearsing possible solutions to problems. But all this mental activity just makes me more anxious and more stressed the more I try to analyze what's happening. This is worrying going wrong and simply creating more anxiety.

Unlike most worriers, I've been privileged enough to be able to conduct more than thirty years of psychological research on why many of us become catastrophic worriers, so I've become very familiar with many different forms of worrying and what causes them. But this knowledge of what causes catastrophic worrying isn't just confined to stuffy academic books; it has provided invaluable information on how we can fix maladaptive forms of worrying that can often lead to chronic mental health problems and lifelong anxiety.

I'll be honest with you from the start: the reasons why people develop catastrophic forms of worrying are complex. Well, that make sense; otherwise, we'd all be able to figure it out and fix it (and I wouldn't have been able to have had a salary researching it for thirty years!). But we now know quite a lot about how catastrophic worrying works. So I'll try to unpack these complex reasons one by one so you can understand the psychological processes that contribute to chronic worrying and you can use this knowledge to help you through the various therapeutic tips this book is offering.

Don't forget: solutions to psychological problems, such as worrying, are likely to be much more successful if you understand the cognitive processes that make you worry. Indeed, in many cases, the insight provided by understanding the psychological causes of your worry can often be enough to provide ways to manage your worrying and anxiety yourself. So please don't take a shortcut and go straight to the tips and exercises. Insight helps because it lets you know how best to invest your efforts and continually bear in mind that any form of uncontrollable and stressful worrying that you experience is learned. I hope the chapters in this book are accessible and engaging and will help you to understand how you learned to worry badly. You can "unlearn" bad worrying and replace it with "smart" worrying that helps you to solve problems rather than dwell unproductively on them.

Let's begin with a little more insight into the worry monster that is catastrophic worrying and reveal some of the features of catastrophizing that you probably didn't know about. Many of these facts will undoubtedly surprise you.

The Catastrophizing Helter-Skelter

WORRY FACT 1. Worriers continue with a catastrophizing sequence of thoughts for much longer than nonworriers—even if the worry is one they will never have worried about before.

WORRY FACT 2. For worriers, aspects of personal inadequacy creep into the catastrophizing stream. These include thoughts such as inability to cope, low self-esteem, and lack of control over events. This happens whether the worry is an old, well-practiced one or a completely new worry.

WORRY FACT 3. Worriers become more and more uncomfortable and anxious as catastrophizing proceeds and regularly end up more anxious and stressed at the end of the process than they were at the start.

WORRY FACT 4. Catastrophic worriers become convinced that the bad things they're worrying about are very likely to happen. This may be because the negative thoughts they generate—both about themselves and their worry—create an "availability bias," which makes negative thoughts more "available" in memory than positive thoughts. They then become biased, thinking that bad or negative things are more common and likely to happen than positive or good things.

I'm going to begin with what may seem like a very unusual example. The Statue of Liberty is a robed female figure representing the Roman goddess Libertas. She is a three-hundred-foot-high neoclassical sculpture and stands on Liberty Island in New York Harbor. She was a gift from the people of France and has stood stoically in the entrance to New York Harbor since her dedication in 1886. She holds a torch above her head and is made primarily of copper. Still baffled? Well, just imagine yourself as this Roman goddess standing in the entrance to New York Harbor—would you be worried about being the Statue of Liberty?

In one of our early studies, we asked "high" and "low" worriers to imagine they were the Statue of Liberty standing in New York Harbor and that they were worried about this.[3] We didn't do this to test their imagination or their knowledge of history! We wanted to see what happened when we asked worriers and nonworriers to worry about something they will almost certainly never have worried about before: Would pathological worriers still worry more than nonworriers about something as hypothetical as being the Statue of Liberty? And would worriers still catastrophize this worry more than nonworriers?

To be able to objectively measure how long worriers and nonworriers would worry about being the Statue of Liberty, we conducted what is known as a catastrophizing interview. This begins with the researcher asking the question, "What is it that worries you about X?" where X is the topic of the worry. If their worry is their finances, we ask them, "What is it that worries you about your finances?" They may reply, "I may lose my home if I can't pay the mortgage." We then pass this response back to them by asking, "What is it that worries you about losing your home if you can't pay the mortgage?" In response to this, the participant may then reply, "I won't be able to take care of my family." We keep throwing the last reply back at the interviewee in the form of "What is it that worries you about (X)," until they can think of no more responses, and then we end the interview.[4] What is useful about this procedure is that we can count the number of questioning steps that someone is able to continue with before they stop and run out of replies. And—surprise, surprise—chronic worriers will usually continue for significantly longer than individuals who worry much less. It's as if the worrier has many more responses to potential worries stored up in their brain than the nonworrier, and this enables them to elaborate their worries in an almost viral fashion.

So, what happens when we conduct the catastrophizing interview with worriers and nonworriers and ask them to worry about being the Statue of Liberty? I've listed some responses given to the Statue of Liberty worry below. This shows the sequences of responses given by someone who scores high on measures of pathological worrying (a "high" worrier) and by someone who scores low on these measures (a "low" worrier). The numbers indicate the sequential responses in the catastrophizing interview.

Catastrophizing sequences from the Statue of Liberty worry interviews:

High worrier:

1. I'm worried about not being able to move

2. That I would be attacked in some way

3. That I would not be able to fight back

4. That I would not be able to control what other people did to me

5. That I would feel inadequate

6. That other people would begin to think I was inadequate

7. That in my relationship with those people, I would not be respected

8. That I would not have any influence over them

9. That other people would not listen to me

10. That it would cause a loss of self-esteem

11. That this loss of self-esteem would have a negative effect on my relationships with others

12. That I would lose friends

13. That I would be alone

14. That I would have no one to talk to

15. Because it would mean that I would not be able to share any thoughts and problems with other people

16. That I would not get advice from others

17. That none of my problems would be adequately sorted out

18. That they would remain and get worse

19. That eventually I would not be able to cope with them

20. That eventually my problems would have more control over me than I had over them

21. That they would prevent me from doing other things

22. That I would be unable to meet new people and make friends

23. That I would be lonely

Low worrier:

1. I can't move

2. I enjoy being free

The obvious difference between the two interview sequences is the number of answers participants have before running out of responses. The high worrier continues the interview for a total of twenty-three steps, generating different responses to each question. In contrast, the low worrier can only generate two responses before quitting. The high worrier is much more willing to elaborate on a worry topic than the low worrier.[5]

But this difference in willingness or ability to embellish on a worry topic is not the only interesting feature of the worry-stream responses listed. Look closely at the kinds of things the catastrophic worrier is saying. It seems as though they are driven to beat themselves up as they think through the worry topic. Even with a worry topic as surreal as being the Statue of Liberty, we can see issues of personal inadequacy ("I would not be able to cope"), low self-esteem ("It would cause a loss of self-esteem"), and a lack of control over events ("Eventually, my problems would have more control over me than I had over them"). Then look at where this iterative process has taken the catastrophic worrier—from thinking about being the Statue of Liberty to being lonely and "unable to meet new people and make friends."

We assume that the catastrophic worrier has never worried before about being the Statue of Liberty (unless they have an extreme form of delusional psychopathology that we hadn't picked up on!), so they would never have practiced catastrophizing this worry before. But it didn't prevent them from iterating the worry for a total of twenty-three steps of "What if…?" reasoning and in the process dragging all kinds of lurking personal inadequacies into their stream of consciousness, transforming an abstract worry into something real and immediate.

The table below (which has been adapted from Michael Vasey and Thomas Borkovec's work) shows another example of an individual chronic worrier's responses in a catastrophizing interview. This time, the worry topic is one that afflicts many worriers at some point in their life: getting good grades in school. But on this occasion, the participant was also asked to rate their feelings of discomfort or distress at that point in the interview (the first column, on a scale of 0 to 100, where 0 is not distressed at all and 100 is extremely distressed) and the likelihood with which they thought the response they'd given would actually happen (the second column, on a scale of 0 to 100, where 0 is not likely to happen at all and 100 is certain to happen).[6]

Catastrophizing the Worry Topic "Getting Good Grades in School"

	Distress	Likelihood
I'll never live up to my expectations.	50	30
I will disappoint myself.	60	100
I'll lose my confidence.	70	50
My loss of confidence would spread to other areas of my life.	70	50
I'd have much less control than I'd like.	75	80
I'll be frightened of facing the unknown.	75	100
I'll become extremely anxious.	75	100
My anxiety would mean I'd lose even more self-confidence.	75	80
I'd never get my confidence back.	75	50
I'll have no control over my life.	75	80

	Distress	Likelihood
I'd be vulnerable to things that usually wouldn't bother me.	75	80
I'd become even more anxious.	80	80
I'd have no control at all, and I'd have mental health problems.	85	30
My whole life would become dependent on drugs and therapy.	50	30
I'd always be dependent on drugs.	85	50
The drugs would ruin my body.	85	100
I'd be constantly in pain.	85	100
I'd die.	90	80
I'd end up in hell.	95	80

In this case, the worrier has catastrophized "getting good grades in school" to ending up in hell—and has gone through drug addiction, physical pain, and mental health problems on the way! Even in this example, we see the same self-bashing responses creeping into the worry stream: personal inadequacy ("I'd be vulnerable to things that normally wouldn't bother me"), low self-esteem ("I will disappoint myself"), and a lack of control over events ("I'd have no control at all, and I'd have mental health problems").

This example also tells us a couple of additional things about the catastrophic worrier. First, the worrier becomes more and more distressed as the catastrophizing process continues (the first column of ratings). This is typical of anyone who has ever catastrophically worried—and I've experienced it myself. The initial purpose of your worrying is to try to reassure yourself in some way that the problem is not as bad as you initially thought, or you may be worrying to think up a solution to deal with it.

But exactly the opposite happens. Instead, you convince yourself that you're probably incapable of dealing with the problem, you identify other potential problems in addition to the original one, and you're significantly more stressed at the end of the worry bout than you were at the start. Now how did that happen? It certainly wasn't what you'd intended.

Secondly, the catastrophizing worrier strongly believes that the bad things they think about in the catastrophizing sequence are very likely to happen (the second column of ratings). In this example, the worrier even ends up believing with some certainty (80 out of 100) that they will die and go to hell—and all this from a starting point of worrying about getting good grades in school.

What is it that convinces the catastrophic worrier that these bad things are likely to happen? It's most likely a variety of factors that are thrown into the mix during the catastrophizing process. For example, the ease with which the worrier is able to generate responses during the catastrophizing interview—most of them negative—testifies to the availability of these negative responses in memory (don't forget, this is very different for the nonworriers, who are often only able to generate a couple of responses). All this negativity is ready to be thrown into the stream of thoughts at the slightest opportunity, bringing reminders of personal inadequacy, inability to cope, and lack of control to the forefront. These factors likely convince the worrier that the bad thing preying on their mind will happen.

In addition, the catastrophizing process generates a flood of negative information. This creates what's known as an "availability bias" when making decisions.[7] For example, seeing several news reports about vehicle thefts is likely to influence your judgments about vehicle theft in your neighborhood—you're likely to believe it is much more common than it really is. Similarly, if your catastrophizing bouts are made up predominantly of negative statements and thoughts, you'll be much more likely to believe that the negative thing you're worrying about is more likely to happen—simply because your estimate of that worrisome outcome actually happening will be directly related to the number of negative thoughts you've been able to drag up related to that worry.

Then there's that rising level of distress throughout the catastrophizing process—this is more grist to the mill. At an unconscious level, the worrier will continually be asking themselves, "Have I successfully dealt with this worry yet?" and in the absence of any real evidence will default to how their mood feels at that particular moment. That mood becomes increasingly negative as the worry bout continues and is telling the worrier, "No, you haven't dealt with it, you're still stressed, so keep worrying!" So by the end of the catastrophizing process, that negative, distressed mood is yelling at the top of its voice, "That bad thing just ain't going away!"—even if that bad thing is something as extreme as a trip to the gates of hell!

Now, at this point we've identified a number of factors associated with catastrophic worrying, but which of these factors are genuine causes (that cause you to catastrophize), and which are simply the consequences of catastrophizing? This is quite an important thing to know in order to manage catastrophizing. Questions to ask include: Do our feelings of personal inadequacy make us catastrophize? Do the feelings of stress and anxiety we experience when worrying cause us to catastrophize for longer? So, let's look at the evidence relating to these two factors. Do poor problem-solving confidence and our negative mood during worrying contribute to the catastrophizing process?

Taking Catastrophizing into the Lab

Many people have an image of a psychologist as a bespectacled therapist sitting in a chair with legs crossed next to a client who is recumbent on a couch. But most psychologists are far removed from that caricature of a Freudian analyst. We are scientists who do experiments. And most often, we do these experiments in laboratories. But don't be alarmed, we're not scalpel-wielding vivisectionists cutting up brains to find the brain's "worry center." In fact, very little is likely to be learned about worrying by cutting up a brain. Unlike medical doctors, psychologists are more interested in what information goes into a brain and, as a consequence, what behavior comes out. By observing these in-out relationships, we can infer what's happening in the middle—in this case, in that lump of grey matter located in your skull, or the "mind" if you prefer to call it that. In the next sections, I'll describe a couple of experiments that are relevant to our discussion of causes and effects during catastrophic worrying.

The Conundrum of the Worrier's Problem-Solving Abilities

WORRY FACT 5. Catastrophic worriers tend to have poor problem-solving confidence even though studies suggest they are as good as anyone at coming up with good solutions for life problems.

WORRY FACT 6. Experimental studies show that the catastrophic worriers' poor problem-solving confidence actually has a causal effect on catastrophizing—the poorer that problem-solving confidence is, the longer the worrier catastrophizes for.

One of the interesting things we investigated early on in our studies of worrying was the problem-solving ability of chronic worriers. Were they poorer at solving problems, and was that why they worried more? If you can come up with a good solution to a challenging life problem, then there's no need to worry, is there? However, even if you can come up with good solutions to life's problems, anxiety sabotages the problem-solving process. Anxiety is usually the trigger for much of our worrying, but it is also associated with a whole variety of cognitive processes that tend to thwart effective problem solving—and I'll describe these processes in more detail in chapter 6.

But anxiety doesn't suddenly make us into bad problem-solvers—it simply takes away our confidence. In one study, we asked eighty-two undergraduate students to complete questionnaires measuring worry frequency and problem-solving confidence, and then we asked them to provide solutions to a variety of real-life problems.[8] Here's an example scenario: "Mr. A. was listening to people speak at a meeting about how to make things better in his neighborhood. He wanted to say something important and become a leader. The story ends with him being elected leader and presenting a speech." The students were asked to write the middle of the story, and their responses were independently assessed for effectiveness. We expected that chronic worriers would score very poorly on the problem-solving task, but this wasn't the case—they were just as good as nonworriers at thinking up ideal solutions for hypothetical life problems. However, what we did find was that the measures of pathological worrying were directly related to measures of poor problem-solving confidence. That is, chronic worriers can think up good solutions but lack the skills or confidence to implement those solutions—a finding reminiscent of the themes of personal inadequacy that come out in the worry-streams of catastrophic worriers.

But does poor problem-solving confidence cause people to catastrophize? This is where the experiments become important. To discover if poor problem-solving confidence makes catastrophizing worse, we needed to manipulate poor problem-solving confidence in the lab and measure its effect on catastrophizing. We took a random sample of volunteers and asked each of them to undertake our catastrophizing interview to see how long they would catastrophize one of their own current worries.[9] But before we did this, we made some of them highly confident of their problem-solving abilities and made others uncertain of their abilities. We did this in a rather sneaky way. We asked all the volunteers to attempt the real-life problem-solving scenarios described in the previous paragraph. Then we gave half of them feedback indicating they had done very well on this, and the other half—you guessed it—were given feedback indicating they'd done very badly (don't worry, everyone was fully debriefed about the deception at the end of the experiment!).

In the subsequent catastrophizing interview, we found that those whose problem-solving confidence was undermined by the false feedback persisted at the catastrophizing task for significantly longer than those who'd had their problem-solving confidence bolstered. It seems that poor problem-solving confidence does indeed cause people to catastrophize for longer—and in our study, this effect couldn't be explained by differences in mood between the two groups. Discovering this causal relationship is important because it means that if we can bolster your problem-solving confidence, that should help shorten individual bouts of worrying and catastrophizing.

So, what happens if we do the same kind of experiment, but this time manipulate mood instead of problem-solving confidence? This kind of experiment is relatively easy to do but had some unexpected results.

Negative Mood: The "Unconscious Worry Motivator"

WORRY FACT 7. Negative moods, such as stress, anxiety, sadness, tiredness, and pain, cause an individual to catastrophize for longer—regardless of whether they are a chronic worrier or not.

WORRY FACT 8. One way that negative mood causes individuals to catastrophize for longer is by activating the systematic processing of information. This is a left-hemisphere brain process that ensures that full and proper thought is given to the worry problem, potentially creating catastrophic scenarios and extending the length of individual worry bouts.

WORRY FACT 9. Mood is often unconsciously used as information to decide whether to end the worry bout or keep worrying. Since most worrying occurs in a negative mood, this negative mood is effectively saying, "No, you're still feeling negative, anxious, or stressed, so you haven't achieved your worry goals yet—so keep on worrying!"

We experience many negative moods—many of them visit us every single day. These negative moods include anxiety, stress, depression, sadness, tiredness, pain, anger, and frustration. But it's almost certain that modern-day human beings wouldn't still experience these moods unless they had some evolutionary benefit, and in almost every case, they have a protective function. I've called them collectively "negative" moods because in their own individual ways, they are not very pleasant emotions to experience—and that, of course, is the way they help us survive.

All these negative moods can influence whether we'll worry and how we'll worry—often in very subtle and indirect ways that we're not consciously aware of.

Think back to a recent news headline you read. Recall that headline as vividly as you can. How did it make you feel? The chances are that it triggered a negative emotional reaction because surveys suggest that over 50 percent of news stories are unambiguously negative, covering stories such as terrorism, crime, war, natural disasters, mass shootings, disease, and famine, while as little as 15 percent of news stories are unambiguously positive.[10] And like me, you may have experienced a flood of unrelenting negative news like this most recently during the coronavirus pandemic of 2020 and 2021.

So how does all this negative news affect us? Given that most people will sample the news at least once every day, we decided to see how it might affect their own levels of worrying, and we did indeed find that watching negative news led to viewers worrying more about their own problems.[11]

We sampled many hours of TV news segments and then edited these samples to produce three different fourteen-minute news roundups to use in our experiment. One consisted solely of unambiguously negative news items (stories about war, crime, famine, and so forth), one was made up entirely of positive news items (people winning the lottery or recovering from serious illness), and the third was made up of news items considered to be emotionally neutral by independent raters. The purpose of this experiment was to see if the emotional valency of these individual news segments affected the way that people catastrophized their own worries.

We showed these news segments to three groups of people, none of whom scored particularly highly on measures of worry. One group watched the negative version, a second group watched the positive version, and the third group watched the neutral version. We then asked them each to participate in a catastrophizing interview to see whether the different news segments affected the length of time they would catastrophize one of their own current worries.

The results were quite clear. The participants who viewed the negative news segment catastrophized their own worries significantly longer and through significantly more steps than participants in either of the other two groups. Remember, the people who took part in this experiment were not selected in any way for their existing levels of worrying, so the results suggest that you don't have to be a chronic worrier for negative news to make you catastrophize more.

These findings are quite robust, and anything that puts you into a negative mood will usually make you catastrophize or worry for longer than if you're in a more positive mood.[12] In the above example, we used negative news to generate a negative mood, and in most cases this negative mood was in the form of sadness or anxiety, but in other experiments, a negative mood was generated in other ways, such as by watching sad films or listening to sad or anxiety-provoking music. In daily life, there are many things that create negative mood—work stress, relationship problems, financial difficulties, health issues. These are just a few examples, and they may be with you day after day, creating a constant state of negative mood that drives your catastrophizing about any worry that's on your mind at the time.

How is it that being in a negative mood makes you catastrophize a worry for longer? There are two particular reasons.

First, let's start with what may seem like a simple question: Who would you most trust to do an important task properly—a task that requires a lot of attention to detail? Someone in a happy or positive mood? Or someone in a negative mood who might be stressed, sad, or even angry?

The answer is that it depends very much on the nature of the task. People in a positive mood are much better at creative tasks, while people in a negative mood are much better at analytical tasks that require collecting and analyzing information, problem solving, and making decisions. For example, psychologist Jeffrey Melton at Indiana University carried out a study investigating the effect of mood on the ability of undergraduate students to solve logical puzzles (such as, "If all A are B, and some B are C, how many of A are C?").[13] Prior to tackling the logical puzzles, half the participants were asked to read *The Far Side* cartoons or listen to a tape of comedian Rodney Dangerfield; the other half were asked to read a boring set of adjectives. Interestingly, the results showed that the positive-mood participants, who were exposed to humorous material, performed significantly worse on the logical puzzles than the group that read boring adjectives.

However, being in a positive mood doesn't impair your analytical skills; it's being in a negative mood that actually focuses performance on tasks with an analytical or problem-solving element. Negative mood triggers cognitive processes that make us examine information and ideas in a step-by-step systematic way, whereas positive mood can often trick us into taking shortcuts by using what are called "heuristics"—mental shortcuts that allow us to make decisions and judgments quickly but may in fact end up being the wrong decisions! For example, imagine a little old lady stops you in the street and asks you to lend her some money. In a negative mood, you're more likely to systematically analyze information about her before deciding to trust her. However, in a positive mood, you're more likely to use a "heuristic" as a shortcut. For example, she may remind you of your grandmother, so you assume she's kind, gentle, and trustworthy—just like your grandmother. On the basis of this shortcut, you decide to trust her—but it may be the wrong decision!

This is all relevant to catastrophic worrying because most worrying tends to take place while you're in a negative mood—and catastrophic worrying is a very analytic process (as we saw in the worry sequences above). Worries are problems that often concern life matters that are either threatening or challenging, so they are likely to be considered while in a negative mood, such as being stressed or anxious. This negative mood immediately activates systematic information processing—which prevents you from using shortcuts such as heuristics to make decisions—and ensures that you consider every detail of your worry, fact by fact, and think through as many potential catastrophic outcomes as you can conjure up.

This all suggests that worrying is a special form of systematic information processing facilitated by negative mood, and in support of this view, worrying and systematic information processing share similar functional brain characteristics.[14] Systematic information processing appears to occur predominantly in the brain's left frontal lobes—where verbal processing of information and many forms of decision-making take place—and worrying is also associated with left-hemisphere activation and verbal processing of information.

So, negative mood facilitates worrying by activating systematic information processing—an activity that will ensure proper and full thought is given to the worry problem, potentially creating catastrophic scenarios and extending the length of individual worry bouts.

Secondly, negative mood has another, rather unexpected, role to play in facilitating worrisome thought. Negative mood makes it harder for you to stop worrying—a role that can make you feel like pathological worrying is uncontrollable.

Here's how this works. The aim of much of our worrying is to consider all eventualities associated with an upcoming problem and to possibly find solutions to this problem. But how do we decide when we've achieved these aims? I've already mentioned that worriers tend to have poor problem-solving confidence, so the worrier may have great difficulty finding objective, evidence-based reasons for believing that their worrying has been successful, that it can be terminated, and that solutions can be implemented at the appropriate time.

So, what kind of information can the worrier use to make decisions about whether their worrying has achieved its aims? Well, one thing that many of us do when we lack objective information to make a decision is to default to our current mood—we allow our mood to determine our decisions. In the case of worrying, a positive mood suggests we've achieved our goals, and a negative mood suggests we haven't.[15]

Since we commonly begin our worrying in a negative mood and this mood state continues for much of the time we're worrying, that negative mood is effectively saying, "No, you're still feeling negative, anxious, or stressed, so you have not achieved your worry goals yet—so keep on worrying!" Using mood as information in this way is not a conscious process, and for many chronic worriers, it is an automatic process honed by many years of regular practice. It's a process that makes your catastrophic worrying seem uncontrollable because you're unaware that it's the information provided by your negative mood that's making you keep persevering with your worrying. Becoming aware of this "mood as information" process is a start to managing it, but we also need to take more direct action to control those negative moods that occur during worrying.

EXERCISE 1: Measuring Your Tendency to Catastrophize

In this chapter, I described some of the processes that give rise to catastrophic worrying. It's characterized by a tendency to persistently explore a worry by generating new answers to "What if…?" questions posed by your worry, and this exercise will give you an opportunity to see just how willing you are to elaborate your worry in a way that is characteristic of catastrophic worrying.

Materials

Pencil or pen

Notebook or Catastrophizing Worksheet (available for download from http://www.newharbinger.com/50348)

What It Is

The catastrophizing interview is designed to assess how long you're willing to analyze your worry and, as a consequence, how likely you are to come up with extreme worst-case scenarios. You can do this exercise on your own, but it's better to recruit a friend to act as your catastrophizing interviewer. They will also be able to help you if you become distressed as you think about your worry.

How Will This Help My Worrying?

This exercise will give you some idea of how much of a catastrophic worrier you are, and the responses you generate during the interview may also be characteristic of catastrophic worriers. If completing this exercise leaves you thinking you may be a catastrophic worrier, don't despair—you will learn good worry habits in chapters 8 and 9.

How to Do It

To begin, open your journal to a blank page or download the Catastrophizing Worksheet.

Now think of a worry that has bothered you in the last week and describe it in five to six words. If you feel that using one of your own worries might be distressing, you can use a hypothetical worry, such as being the Statue of Liberty (the example described earlier in this chapter). Write the worry topic at the top of your response sheet (in the case of choosing the Statue of Liberty worry, simply write "Being the Statue of Liberty").

Your interviewer will then ask you a series of questions during the interview (or you will ask yourself if you're on your own), each of which will begin with the phrase "What is it that worries you about...?" Write your response to this in the "reply" line below the question. An example sequence is provided in the "Tips" section.

Continue with this sequence of questions and replies until you cannot think of any further responses or you find yourself repeating the same response three or more times. Your journal entry will look like the following:

Worry topic:

What is it that worries you about your worry topic?

Reply:

What is it that worries you about that?

Reply:

What is it that worries you about that?

Reply:

What is it that worries you about that?

Reply:

After you have completed the catastrophizing interview, answer the following questions:

How many steps did you complete in the interview before deciding to stop?

Take a look at the responses you generated during the various steps of the catastrophizing interview. Were there any responses that reflected issues related to lack of control over events, lack of confidence, or low self-esteem? If so, all these issues can maintain the catastrophizing process.

TIPS

Here's an example interview sequence:

Worry topic: Losing my job

What is it that worries you about losing your job?

Response: I will have no money.

What is it that worries you about having no money?

Response: I will not be able to pay the mortgage.

What is it that worries you about not being able to pay the mortgage?

Response: I will not have anywhere to live.

What is it that worries you about not having anywhere to live?

Response: I'll be homeless and living on the street.

- Our research suggests that if you completed more than twelve steps before stopping, you are probably analyzing your worries a little too much and as a consequence at risk of generating imagined catastrophic outcomes to your worry that may never happen.

- If you frequently experience intense anxiety or stress when worrying, it is best to do this exercise with a friend or relative who can help and support you in case you begin to feel distressed.

- Do not chose a worry to catastrophize that is highly likely to become distressing, and if you prefer, you can use a hypothetical worry (such as being the Statue of Liberty, that we discussed earlier in this chapter) instead of one of your own worries. The procedure will work just as well regardless of whether the worry is real or hypothetical.

- If completing the catastrophizing interview made you feel anxious or stressed, you can use exercise 6 (in chapter 6) and exercise 16 (in chapter 10), which are designed to help you lift your mood and relieve stress.

Reviewing Catastrophizing

This chapter described a number of factors that contribute to catastrophic worrying, and you can review these by looking back at worry facts in this chapter. Making mountains out of molehills is a very common form of pathological worrying that makes the worrier feel their worrying is out of control and simply makes them more and more stressed as worrying continues.

CHAPTER 2

The Origins of Worrying

What Made You a Catastrophic Worrier?

Roadmap of the chapter. Where does chronic and catastrophic worrying come from? What is it that turns some of us into lifelong worrywarts? In this chapter, we'll look closely at the claim by many worriers that they were born that way. The available evidence suggests they probably weren't. Well-researched alternative causes of worrying point to the developmental experiences we may have during childhood—experiences that generate attachment problems and parenting styles that may leave us believing the world is a dangerous and unpredictable place that we need to be continually prepared to face. We'll investigate the roles of negative life events as a risk factor for adult worrying and possible diversities in brain function and cognitive abilities that could facilitate dysfunctional forms of worrying. We end the chapter with an exercise designed to help parents develop confident children who will be less prone to pathological worrying in adulthood.

"You know me, I'm a born worrier."

That's a very blunt statement, and one you'll see many times in this book. It's the chronic worrier's favorite saying, and maybe you've even uttered those words yourself. But are people born worriers? Are there newborn babies popping out of the womb with furrowed brows asking scores of agonizing "What if...?" questions? Maybe there are—but not because they were born to worry. As we'll see in this chapter, there is no single gene for worrying, and genetic studies of worrying indicate that the genetic component of anxiety traits that leads to worrying is modest at best. However, there is one thing that we can say is definitely true, and that is that chronic worriers usually have no recollection of when they started to become worriers. It seems to them that they've been worriers for as long as they can remember. But most of the evidence strongly suggests that there are life events and developmental factors that contribute to chronic and catastrophic worrying, suggesting that in most cases, chronic worrying is acquired during a person's lifetime and is not something immutably passed on in their genes. Let's look through the genetic evidence on this first.

The "Born Worrier" Fallacy

WORRY FACT 1. There are no genetic studies to date that have specifically investigated the heritability of catastrophic or pathological worrying.

WORRY FACT 2. However, the heritability of anxiety-like traits and conditions, such as generalized anxiety disorder (a condition characterized by pathological worrying, discussed in more detail in chapter 4), is consistently around 30 percent.

WORRY FACT 3. Studies of the heritability of anxiety-related traits suggest that the majority of the variance in anxiety levels is the result of environmental factors (experiences) rather than hardwired genetic factors.

It's simply not easy to separate psychological traits into either inherited or learned. This is because genetic factors can influence learning, and experiential factors can influence the expression of individual inherited genes. So the complex interaction between these factors makes it impossible to split a trait exclusively into chunks that represent either nature or nurture.

Let's begin with a hypothetical example. Heritability is often expressed on a percentage scale. But what does it mean to say that worrying is, say, 50 percent inherited? It categorically *doesn't* mean that 50 percent of the reason you worry is due to your genes. It means that 50 percent of the *variability* in worrying in a population can be attributed to genetic factors.

This concept is often difficult to grasp, so let me explain it further with an example. If all human beings were genetically identical—let's say we were living in a world where everyone was cloned from the same set of genes—then everyone would share exactly the same genes. But what if levels of worrying still varied significantly between individuals in this brave new world? In this example, all the variation in worry levels would be environmental because everyone would share exactly the same genes. In this case, the heritability of worrying would be zero, so the variability in worry levels would be due to experienced environmental factors.

So, let's ask the heritability question in a slightly different way. Worry levels vary considerably between human beings, but what percentage of this variability can be attributed to differences in the genes that we inherit?

There are no detailed studies available that have investigated the heritability of worrying as such, but there are many studies that have investigated the heritability of anxiety generally and of generalized anxiety disorder (GAD) in particular—the latter is an anxiety-based problem whose defining characteristic is pathological and catastrophic worrying.

Using a variety of different methodologies, the heritability of anxiety and GAD is usually found to be between 26 and 31 percent.[16] This means that around 30 percent of the variability in anxiety levels within a population can be attributed to genetic factors, suggesting that genetic variability may account for a moderate proportion of anxiety-related traits, but that the remaining majority percentage of the variability must be due to other factors—such as differences in environments and experiences.

If at least some of the variability in levels of anxiety is the result of genetic factors, what is it that's inherited? Genome-wide association studies (GWAS) scan the genomes from many different people looking for genes that predict the presence of individual traits, and these studies have identified some of the genes that underpin anxiety-based problems. But these genes appear to be associated with a vulnerability to very generalized traits, such as a tendency to anxiety disorders generally (rather than to specific anxiety disorders, such as GAD), to depression (which is often comorbid with anxiety), and to neuroticism (a tendency to experience negative moods generally, such as anxiety, anger, irritability, emotional instability, and depression).[17] There's no mention of worry as a specific trait associated with these generalized, anxiety-related vulnerabilities.

So for example, if one of your parents has been diagnosed with GAD, then there's a slightly higher probablity that you'll be diagnosed with an anxiety problem—but that could be any of the anxiety disorders, and not necessarily GAD. No specific genes have been found that are linked to pathological worry explicitly, and in the case of anxiety-related traits, the majority of the variability in these traits appears to be the result of environmental factors that may reflect the effects of developmental experiences, individual traumas, or adverse socioeconomic conditions.

The take-home message is that the legend of the "born worrier" is not backed up by the facts. But this is not a bad thing. If we can show that catastrophic worrying is acquired during the individual's lifetime and is a learned rather than inherited characteristic, then what is learned can also be unlearned, providing hope for the catastrophic worrier that their affliction can be relieved with a bit of hard work and support. Let's look at this evidence next.

The Origins of Anxiety-Related Worry

So, what kind of experiences might turn you into a chronic, catastrophic worrier?

John Bowlby was a British psychologist famous for his interest in childhood development and for his pioneering work on attachment theory. He firmly believed that childhood anxiety stemmed from concerns about parental availability, and his own early life is brimming with examples of parental absence and neglect.

Bowlby was born in 1907, and as a young child, he saw his mother only one hour a day after teatime (lest young Bowlby become spoiled—it was a common view of the British upper classes at the time that too much parental contact would spoil a child). In 1914, his father left to fight in the First World War, coming home briefly only once or twice a year. Even Bowlby's beloved nanny, Minnie, left the family when he was four; he described it later as the tragic loss of a mother figure. Then he was sent off to boarding school, a period of his life that he described as a "terrible time" in his 1973 book, *Separation: Anxiety and Anger*.[18] "I wouldn't send a dog away to boarding school at age seven," he was later to claim. Bowlby's own childhood experiences led to his interest in attachment and emotions, and studies soon began to identify the significant role that attachment, or lack of it, could play in nurturing anxiety and worrying.

Risk factors for catastrophic worrying fall into three distinct categories: attachment and parenting style, negative life events, and diversities in brain function. Children are programmed to learn hard and fast about how to negotiate the world, so what messages does someone like a young John Bowlby take from inconsistent and often absent parenting? The overriding message is "Be prepared"—in other words, anticipate bad things happening by worrying!

The Role of Attachment

WORRY FACT 4. Attachment anxiety and avoidance have regularly been shown to be associated with higher levels of worrying—often as a result of inconsistent or neglectful parenting.

WORRY FACT 5. Intolerance of uncertainty may play a key role in the relationship between adult attachment difficulties and subsequent chronic worrying.

Human beings are social animals, so we all experience feelings of attachment to significant people in our lives. These may be siblings, friends, or partners, but the most meaningful of these significant others are usually the parents who rear us and care for us through childhood into adulthood.

Attachment Types

Attachment anxiety. A type of attachment in which the child experiences anxiety about relationships with significant others, such as parents, friends, or partners. This form of attachment may stem in part from negative, harsh, or inconsistent parenting.

Attachment avoidance. An attachment style that tends to develop in children who do not experience sensitive responses to their needs. The children may grow up to be physically and emotionally independent.

Maternal role reversal. A parent-child relationship that puts the child in the position of the parent by having to look after the parent in some way.

Enmeshment. A form of attachment in which the parent's life and worth are defined in terms of the child's own happiness or pain, success, or failure.

Inconsistent parenting can generate two particular types of insecure attachment—attachment anxiety and attachment avoidance. Anxious-avoidant children are often rejected by their parents and avoid relationships because of the anxiety that was experienced with the rejecting parents. As adults, individuals with this insecure attachment style often develop hyper-vigilance for threats—especially potential attachment threats—and may perceive others as untrustworthy. Their experience of inconsistent parenting disrupts their ability to regulate emotional experiences and lowers their feelings of self-worth, which in turn generates a belief that they are not competent enough to deal with threats and uncertainty.[19]

Characteristics of anxious-avoidant behavior can be found in the catastrophic worrier—namely, a lack of confidence in their ability to cope with threats and challenges, inability to tolerate distress, hypervigilance and attentional biases toward threats, and an intolerance of uncertainty. But is this just coincidence, or can we identify a relationship between inconsistent parenting and subsequent chronic worrying in the child?

There is plenty of evidence that there is a relationship. Attachment anxiety and avoidance have regularly been shown to be associated with higher levels of worrying, and recent studies have also shown an important relationship between anxious and avoidant attachment and intolerance of uncertainty (which we'll look at in more detail in chapter 7). Intolerance of uncertainty is a psychological aversion to uncertainty and is a significant cause of chronic and catastrophic worrying as the worrier attempts to use an iterative worry style to eliminate all possible sources of uncertainty in a worry.[20] This view is further reinforced by a recent study of 290 adults by Gavin Clark and colleagues at the University of New England in Australia.[21] This study suggested that intolerance of uncertainty may play a key role in mediating the relationship between adult-attachment difficulties and subsequent chronic worrying, providing the link by which inconsistent parenting styles may give rise to maladaptive worry strategies in adulthood.

Let's not beat about the bush. Inconsistent parenting has a lot to answer for when it comes to generating childhood anxiety and adult worrying. It's not just absent parenting that's been associated with subsequent adult worrying, but also intrusive parenting and harsh and controlling parenting.[22] Children who receive parenting that is highly controlling and negative (characterised by harsh discipline) and are subjected to strict rules and high expectations from their parents also exhibit increased symptoms of pathological worrying in general and a diagnosis of GAD in particular.[23] The messages that children may take into adulthood from these experiences include that they're incapable of handling challenges and threats on their own and that they're unable to cope with negative events and the emotional reactions these elicit. Overprotective or overcontrolling parenting is also likely to undermine the child's emotional development, leading to emotion regulation difficulties and subsequent anxiety.[24] All are grist to the worry mill later in life.

There is one final set of parenting experiences that have been associated with later adult worrying, and they are maternal role reversal and enmeshment.[25] Role reversal puts the child in the position of being the adult in the parent-child relationship (sometimes known as "parentification"). This may involve the child looking after a sick relative, paying bills, or providing assistance to young siblings. In contrast, enmeshment describes a style of parenting where the parent's life and worth are defined in terms of the child's own happiness or pain, success or failure—the child is the center of the parent's life and the sole purpose of the parent's life. With both maternal role reversal and enmeshment, the child is likely to grow up feeling responsible for the feelings of others, have problems in their adult relationships, and continually seek to ensure that they themselves are prepared for threats and challenges that may adversely affect the physical and emotional needs of others. That's quite a significant worry workload!

It's a tough job being a parent, so let's not just heap blame on Mom and Dad. Many of the circumstances that give rise to inconsistent or extreme parenting may not be factors that are easily within the control of those parents. Factors such as poverty, civil strife, physical illness, and even poor mental health suffered by parents themselves may make optimal parenting difficult or impossible. While we know that insecure attachment is one of the factors that can give rise to chronic worrying in adult life, the conditions that foster insecure attachment may have direct effects on adult anxiety and worrying (we shouldn't rule out the direct influence of poverty, strife, or illness on worry frequency in later life) if only because such factors are replete with the threats and challenges that are the basic fuel for anxiety and worry. I'll talk more about the role of negative life events later in this chapter.

However, the damage is far from irreparably done, and if you view yourself as a worrier who may have evolved from one of these developmental processes, the exercises in part 2 can help you replace pathological and distressing worry with more practically oriented problem-solving approaches to your worries.

Helicopter, Snowplow, and Bubble-Wrap Parenting

WORRY FACT 6. Overprotective parenting, such as helicopter and snow-plow parenting, appears to make the child more vulnerable to anxiety and worry by increasing the child's perception of threat, reducing their perceived control over threat, and increasing their avoidance of threat.

When it comes to bringing up children, there are many things that parents would like to do for their children, but because of circumstances, they simply can't—and their children's mental health may suffer as a result. On the other side of the coin, there are those parents who are overly diligent and simply go overboard with their attention and protection. This parenting style can also produce anxious, worrisome children who often become anxious, worrisome adults.

As standards of living rise, many parents find themselves in a position where they are financially and socially able to micromanage the lives of their offspring, providing extracurricular activities, monitoring social activities, controlling food intake, and providing technologically sophisticated protections against any dangers that the outside world might pose. Most modern-day moms and dads can ensure that location services are constantly active on little Liam's smartphone, but some will often take this to extremes by employing devices such as drones to watch Olivia walk to school![26]

Micromanaging parents are known as "helicopter parents" and are a modern-world phenomenon. They are constantly searching the internet for "better" ways of parenting, using technology to monitor their offspring's every move, and paying particularly close and cosseting attention to their child's education progress. But while our helicopter parents are spending their time monitoring their children's activities, the "snowplow parent" takes it further, plowing onward before their child, actively removing everything in life that might be a potential obstacle before their child encounters it.

What's this got to do with worrying? Well, parents bring many different characteristics to their parenting, and one of the characteristics that appears to facilitate child anxiety and worry is overprotectiveness. Overanxious or overprotective parenting generates a lack of confidence and feelings of inadequacy in a child. Studies carried out by psychologist Ron Rapee and colleagues at Macquarie University in Australia cleverly demonstrated that when mother and child are jointly engaged in a puzzle task, overprotective or anxious mothers are significantly more likely to be intrusive and become overly involved with the child in order to reduce the child's distress. This over-involvement increases the child's vulnerability to anxiety by increasing the child's perception of threat, reducing their perceived control over threat, and increasing their avoidance of threat.[27] Being a mother and doing the right thing for your child is clearly a thankless task!

Ron Rapee has argued that overprotective parents may regularly, but inadvertently, support, assist in, or reward their children's anxious, worrisome, or avoidant behavior—allowing a child to stay home from a social event or school when they're feeling anxious or fearful, reducing a child's distress with special treatment, or bringing toys inside if there's a feared dog present, for example. Such acts may well encourage children to continue to be anxious in order to receive comfort from their parents or avoid situations that make them fearful.

If you think you may be an overprotective parent, I've included an exercise at the end of this chapter designed to help you set your child on the road to being a confident kid for whom coping and not worrying will be their first response to challenges in life.

Finally, we've known for decades that anxiety seems to run in families, with over 80 percent of parents of children with anxiety problems exhibiting significant levels of anxiety themselves.[28] Given that genetic inheritance is not an overwhelming contributor to the variance in our anxiety and worry levels, this strongly suggests that anxiety and worry may somehow be socially "transmitted" within the family.

In an early study, Peter Muris, professor of child psychology at Maastricht University, asked mothers the extent to which they generally expressed their worries in the presence of their children. He found that mothers who always reported expressing their worries in their children's presence had children with the highest levels of self-reported fearful worries.

Every year, around 130 million children are born worldwide to parents who have relatively little experience of parenting and probably even less knowledge about how to protect the mental health of their offspring. The internet provides a confusing manual, and to be safe and sure, overprotective parents often end up protecting their children from the bad things out there rather than teaching them how to cope with them—and as we've seen in chapter 1, poor problem-solving and coping confidence is a causal factor in pathological worrying.

Experiencing Negative Life Events

WORRY FACT 7. A history of negative life events can lead to the development of chronic worrying. Negative and distressing life events will always tip a person into viewing the world as an unpredictable and dangerous place, which generates worry and worrisome intrusive thoughts.

While parenting style can have an important influence on whether you become a worrier or not, another significant factor is experiencing unexpected negative life events. For those with a diagnosis of GAD, there is often a history of negative life events. The severity of their worry-based symptoms is associated with the severity of these negative life events, and uncontrollable worry is also exacerbated in periods immediately following negative life events.[29] To illustrate this, let me introduce you to Jim.

Jim is a fifty-four-year-old man who went to see his doctor about feeling anxious and depressed. He was unable to shake off worries about many topics, including family relationships, housing, and health issues. He believed he'd "always been a worrier," but things got worse as a result of a series of negative life events. He'd had a stressful time in his job as a senior accountant, he injured his back and was retired on medical grounds, his wife left him, and his teenage daughter began avoiding schoolwork. He then began to find decision making difficult and worried over every eventuality. Should he move to a bungalow to help his mobility problems, how could he repair the relationship with his wife, how should he occupy his time now that he was retired, and how could he encourage his daughter to pursue her schoolwork? He began to feel that these worries would drive him mad, seriously damage his health, or send him into deep depression. Jim's childhood and adolescence included an unaffectionate father who praised him only after achieving perfect school performances and an anxious mother who saw potential disaster everywhere. Jim gradually developed beliefs about himself as unlovable, other people as generally critical of him, and the world as a dangerous place. Subsequent psychological assessment confirmed Jim with a diagnosis of GAD.[30]

Poor Jim. An anxious mother alerts him to the dangers that lurk in the world; an unaffectionate father's behavior leads Jim to believe he is unlovable and that others are generally critical of him. Then, in a short period of time, a series of negative events fills his life. His perception of himself as inadequate prevents him from coping and finding suitable solutions to his problems. Yet, worrying is seen as a necessary activity but is distressingly uncontrollable and unproductive. Negative and distressing life events will always tip a person into viewing the world as an unpredictable and dangerous place, which generates worry and worrisome intrusive thoughts about these negative events. But often, this view of the world may only be temporary and lifts as better times ensue. In contrast, many other individuals who become pathological worriers have a chronic history of negative life events, including physical and psychological abuse and parental neglect, and for their whole lifetime, they will have the view that the world is a dangerous, threatening, and unpredictable place that they need to be constantly wary of.

What's Going On in the Brain?

WORRY FACT 8. Brain-scan studies show that activity in the prefontal brain region—an area of the brain involved in planning and decision making—is associated with symptoms of GAD and chronic worrying.

WORRY FACT 9. Individuals with a diagnosis of autism are particularly prone to pathological and catastrophic worrying.

WORRY FACT 10. Potentially any diversity in higher brain function that limits the ability to control and manage thoughts and to regulate emotions is a potential risk factor for uncontrolled, distressing worrying.

Because worrying is a cognitive, thought-based activity, we may tend to believe that an explanation of worrying lies in an understanding of the brain. Neuroscientists use elaborate equipment costing millions of dollars to research how the brain works. Surely, this will provide the ultimate explanation, right? Well, probably not—expensive research doesn't always provide the answers, and with a psychological phenomenon like worrying, an understanding of that activity is probably better couched in terms of emergent properties of the brain, such as cognitions and beliefs, rather than a description of the neural pathways in the brain.

But let's not impulsively throw out the neuroscience baby with the bathwater. Is there anything that neuroscience has to say about worrying? There is some evidence, but it's not particularly revealing. For example, brain-scan studies show that activity in the prefontal brain regions is associated with symptoms of GAD.[31] But this is not a surprising finding because these brain areas are associated with a range of complex cognitive processes, including planning and decision making, all of which would be important components of worrisome thought.

All that tells us is that the prefrontal cortex is probably where worrying takes place in the brain, but such studies have not really provided any convincing explanation of why worrying in pathological worriers can be so extreme, distressing, and uncontrollable. One possibility from neuroscience that hints at why pathological worrying is so distressing is that GAD appears to be associated with abnormalities in emotional regulation. Such studies suggest that individuals with GAD have a reduced capacity for emotional regulation,[32] a characteristic that may contribute to difficulties in coping with threats and challenges.

In addition, some of the core characteristics of autism may make individuals with a diagnosis of autism particularly prone to pathological and catastrophic worrying. The argument here is that the core characteristics of autism, such as a preference for sameness and routines and a difficulty adjusting to change that may generate an intolerance of uncertainty, may be fundamental risk factors for pathological and distressing worrying.

Even high-functioning autism can be associated with diversities in brain function that can create a risk for intolerance of uncertainty. These neurological diversities include poor working-memory capacity (an inability to hold information in mind while executing other cognitive tasks), impairments in executive functioning (causing difficulties in planning and decision making), and difficulties in global processing (difficulties putting events into context and "getting the bigger picture"). It's also associated with problems of "top-down" control of mental processes, such that individuals with autism may find it difficult to consciously control mental processes (such as intrusive thoughts), to inhibit thoughts and mental processes, and as a consequence, to be relatively unable to regulate the negative emotions that are often an outcome of mental processes, such as worrying.

So while intolerance of uncertainty may drive the individual with autism to try to mentally deal with all problems that may have an element of uncertainty, their attempts may regularly fail because of their lack of control over both mental activities that are important in this context and their difficulties regulating emotional responses (causing distress). The result is that worrying fails to deal with problems successfully and becomes a cause of distress. However, there's been a good deal of research on these autism-related, anxiety-based problems in recent years, and we can be optimistic that new therapeutic interventions will be developed soon that are specifically designed to help alleviate them.

But it's not just a diagnosis of autism that comes with this risk factor for worrying. Potentially, any diversity in higher brain function that limits the ability to control and manage thoughts and to regulate emotions is a potential risk factor for uncontrolled, distressing worrying. The research on this at present is slim, but there is every possibility that neuroscience research in the future may be able to identify diversities in brain function that directly contribute to pathological, catastrophic, chronic, and distressing worrying.

This is important because, while I've placed the emphasis on developmental and experiential factors as causes of pathological worrying, there may be other biological factors that make worrisome thinking difficult, uncontrollable, unsuccessful, and distressing. These biological factors do not necessarily need to be genetically inherited, but in many cases may be the result of either pre- or postnatal abnormalities in brain development caused by environmental stressors, such as abnormal brain development in-utero or in the elderly through age-related neurological deterioration as the brain ages.[33]

Teach Your Children Well

In this chapter, we looked closely at developmental and experiential factors that give rise to chronic worrying in adulthood. Many of these factors relate to styles of parenting, and in particular, overprotective parenting. This parenting style is often practiced by parents who themselves are anxious and wary of the world as a threatening place and believe they are doing the right thing by protecting their children from all possible dangers, threats, and challenges.

But overprotective parenting tends to create kids who lack confidence and have failed to learn useful coping strategies. This is because their parents have not allowed them to confront challenges in their lives and learn how to deal with them, and individuals who lack confidence in their ability to deal with threats and challenges end up becoming anxious worriers.

So, what can you do as a parent? Many anxious parents have had little experience treading the line between "protective" parenting (good) and "overprotective" parenting (not so good) so find it very difficult to know exactly what to do. The following exercise provides some simple advice on how you might help your children become confident kids—a confidence that may foster an ability to actively cope with the travails of life rather than simply worrying about them.

EXERCISE 2: Creating Confident Children

One of my colleagues at the University of Sussex is Professor Sam Cartwright-Hatton, and she has spent many years developing programs to help parents raise confident children who are encouraged to develop coping skills that minimize their anxiety and worrying. In this exercise, I'll describe some of the ideas she uses in her practice, Flourishing Families Clinic.[34] Another excellent source of tips for developing independent children who can overcome worrying is the book *Helping Your Child with Fears and Worries* by University of Reading (UK) clinical psychologists Cathy Creswell and Lucy Willetts.[35] I've also summarized some of their tips here.

Materials

None

What It Is

We know that anxious kids often think, *I can't cope with anything,* so what does a confident kid need to think instead? In this exercise, I'll describe a series of tips for activities to help your children develop self-confidence, independence, and a sense of being able to cope.

How Will This Help My Child's Worrying?

Many individuals who lack confidence in their ability to deal with threats and challenges end up becoming anxious worriers, so providing your children with activities that develop their self-confidence and ability to cope with tasks will help to protect them against becoming chronic worriers in adulthood.

How to Do It

A confident kid needs to develop a set of confidence beliefs and also think confident thoughts. These are attributes that are largely developed through experience. Don't forget, as a parent, you are ideally situated to provide some of these experiences for your child, and here are some general examples of how you can provide these activities. Think about how you might be able to integrate some of these activities into the daily life of your family.

- Get your child to "have a go" at either being independent or doing "grown-up" things. A good start here can be to have your child do everyday tasks and activities that might allow them to feel grown-up and independent. For younger children (aged, say, six or seven), this could include tidying their bedroom, setting the dinner table, loading the dishwasher, or a task involved with looking after a pet. For older children (over eleven), this could include finding some helpful family information on the internet or getting items from the local store.

- As well as experiencing situations in which they have to cope, most children also need to develop a belief that they can cope. There are a number of ways in which parents can help here. The first is by providing *praise*. Always praise your child for trying and don't forget to ask them how they think they did with the tasks you gave them so they can internalize the successful outcome (*"You did that without any help! Wonderful!"*).

- The second way to foster beliefs about coping is to help your child to *feel respected*. Feeling respected is good for mental health generally and for coping confidence in particular. As a parent, you can model respectfulness with your actions by using pleasant tones and positive language and not interrupting what your child is saying or doing.

- It's inevitable that your child will worry about things, but a parent can help turn worries into problem solving. Whatever it is your child is worried about, try to devise a plan that can be put in place if the worry actually happens (but don't forget, most worries don't happen!—see chapter 5). If you devise a plan that you can share with your child, then they are likely to feel a greater sense of control than if you simply tell them to "stop worrying!" The latter will feel to them like you're simply abandoning them to the things they're anxious about.

- Children are relatively new to the world, so there is likely to be much they are unsure about until they acquire experience of the world. It will seem like a place full of uncertainties. But, as I'll point out in more detail in chapter 7, an intolerance of uncertainty is a colossal risk factor for catastrophic worrying, so getting your child used to accepting uncertainty is important. You can start by not springing things on your child out of the blue. Otherwise, they may begin to believe that nasty things can happen at any time without warning. Eventually, you may want to introduce them to uncertainty in a measured way, perhaps by introducing a new element into a well-practiced routine (for example, by taking a slightly different route home from school or by putting something different into their lunchbox). Remember, pleasant surprises will introduce them to uncertainty in a very positive rather than negative way.

TIPS

Here are some tips for helping your child successfully engage with independent activities.

- Talk them through the activity first or even show them what to do by acting it out yourself.

- Together with your child, make a record of what activities they completed successfully.

- Break difficult tasks down into small steps.

- Stay calm. Don't show your anxieties if your child is getting stressed.

- Praise your child for aspects of the task they've completed successfully.

- Don't be overprotective—don't keep intervening in the activity, especially if your child is working effectively on the task.

- Try to avoid using overprotective phrases such as "Be careful!" or "Don't hurt yourself."

The Origins of Being a Lifelong Worrier

In this chapter, we looked at the potential factors that produce the chronic and catastrophic worrier. The available evidence suggests that genetics may only be a moderate contributor, with a heritability score of around 30 percent toward factors like anxiety generally and the worry disorder called generalized anxiety disorder specifically. This, of course, suggests that worriers are unlikely to be the surefire "born worrier" they regularly claim they are.

Some important sources for pathological worrying in adulthood are developmental and experiential ones. I identified attachment issues—such as insecure and anxious attachment—and the role of parenting, especially neglectful, inconsistent, and even overprotective parenting. Experiencing negative life events can also lead to chronic worrying—either in the short term following a period of negative life events or over the longer term for individuals with a history of negative life events, which may include physical and psychological abuse and prolonged parental neglect.

Finally, to date, there is little evidence available from neuroscience studies that casts light on the origins of pathological and catastrophic worrying. But diversities in brain function that adversely affect an individual's ability to control and manage their thoughts, to regulate their emotions, and to be an effective planner and decision-maker may play a role in chronic, dysfunctional worrying.

CHAPTER 3

The Worries of
the World

*What Do People
Catastrophize About?*

Roadmap of the chapter. What do people worry about? To be honest, worriers will worry about absolutely anything—and if you're a chronic worrier, you'll worry about "absolutely anything" for longer and with more distress than a nonworrier. In this chapter, we'll first explore the traditional topics of worry, such as health, finances, work, and relationships, and then move on to consider the catastrophizing of daily hassles, many of which have become features of our lives only in the last few decades. Finally, we'll discuss modern worries created by recent technological developments, such as the internet, social media, and twenty-four-hour news consumption. In this chapter, you'll find an exercise for measuring your worry domains, and if you feel overwhelmed by negative news and the worries it creates, there's also an exercise on managing your news consumption.

WORRY FACT 1. Chronic worriers can usually catastrophize any kind of worry, and this is often because they lack the knowledge to make an objective assessment of the risk posed by their worry.

WORRY FACT 2. Worrying is significantly higher in individuals with a diagnosed anxiety disorder, and this is usually because the fear that drives their anxiety becomes a primary source of worrying.

What do leaky plumbing, nuclear holocausts, and parking problems all have in common? Yes, you guessed right—they're all things that someone at some time has worried about. *The Hunger Games* star Jennifer Lawrence worries about her private details being made public, actress Amanda Seyfried worries about her dog opening the apartment window and falling out, and singer-songwriter Adele gets so worried about going on stage that she's physically sick before performances.

I'm the leaky plumbing worrier. My bête noire is lying awake in the middle of the night wondering if the central heating system is leaking (here in the UK, most central heating systems are water-based). But in the silent blackness of the early hours, I'm not satisfied with just worrying about that. My "What if...?" brain has catastrophized this into a flood that has collapsed the ceiling in my study, trashed my computer, and corrupted all my precious computer files. Oh, the devastation caused by leaky plumbing! But wait, this has never actually happened to me—but for some reason, it doesn't stop me thinking it might.

My real-life experience of leaky plumbing is that I rarely get leaks in my central heating, and when I do, I normally spot the leak, call a plumber, and get it fixed without any flooding or water damage. But my real-life experiences amount to nothing when my worry brain is churning out the "What if...?" scenarios at three o'clock in the morning.

This inability to appreciate the testimony of our own previous experiences reminds me of a man referred to as Mr. H., who had been worrying about the inevitability of nuclear oblivion every day for over thirty years. Each news broadcast and each newspaper headline sent him into cascades of catastrophic worrying about nuclear war. The mere mention of the word "Russia" or "China" would trigger a panic attack and the belief that nuclear war was imminent and he would be consumed by the searing heat of a nuclear attack. His suffering was triggered every day by catching news headlines that sparked his anxieties about nuclear war—yet every day for thirty years, he survived, merely to experience his worry again the very next day.

In such cases, worry has no respect for previous experience. It triggers your brain into catastrophic thought as though each day were the first day of your life. At least Phil Connors, the resilient reporter in the film *Groundhog Day*, learned lessons from each of his Groundhog Day experiences—sadly, many chronic worriers do not.

So, what is it about hypothetical worries that we've never experienced before that cause us so much continuous grief? At least part of the problem is that when we create hypothetical worries, we often don't understand them fully enough to do a proper risk assessment. I know nothing about plumbing, so I have no means of determining whether a small leak in my central heating is likely to burst into a computer-trashing flood. If I did know about plumbing, I might be less inclined to catastrophize potential leaks. Similarly, Mr. H. had become phobic of the news and so avoided any details that went beyond simple headlines. But one consequence of this was that he had very little knowledge of international affairs, so he had no context to assess the likelihood of a nuclear war. The moral here is that it's always a good idea to try to understand your worries and what you can do to either actively assess any risks or find a solution to resolve the worry (if possible). This is the essence of smart worrying and good problem solving, which I'll describe in chapter 9.

These examples indicate that a worry is often out of proportion to the objective reality of the threat posed, and this is often the case when someone has a specific anxiety condition, such as a phobia, obsessive-compulsive disorder, social anxiety, or panic symptoms. Levels of pathological worrying are always elevated in individuals with anxiety disorders because their anxiety is usually driven by a heightened tendency to see things as potential threats, which in turn creates worries.[36]

I'll talk more about anxiety disorders in the next chapter, but if you do suffer an anxiety disorder, the fears that feed your disorder will form the content of many of your worrisome thoughts, you'll catastrophize those thoughts into hypothetical catastrophic outcomes, and often you'll be unable to assess the true risk that these worries pose. Fortunately, most anxiety disorders respond well to psychological therapies, such as cognitive behavioral therapy (CBT) in which the therapist engages the worrier in exercises to help them get objective insight into the risk that their worries actually pose. Usually, the risk posed by these types of worries is very low, often close to zero, and an objective risk-assessment exercise can be helpful even to the sufferer who is aware that their anxieties and fears are irrational.

Traditional Worries

WORRY FACT 3. Traditional worries tend to group around familiar domains that include relationships, finances, work, and health.

WORRY FACT 4. The nature of our traditional topics of worry can evolve and change as the world around us changes to create new angles on what we worry about within the traditional worry domains.

Worriers can literally worry about anything. We saw this in chapter 1 when we asked worriers to worry about being the Statue of Liberty. And they did just that. They spent more time worrying about this than nonworriers, found more negative consequences to being the Statue of Liberty than nonworriers, and beat themselves up in the process by dragging up personal inadequacies and low self-esteem.

But can we make any general statements about the kinds of things that people will tend to worry about? Do we worry about some things more than others?

Psychologists and psychiatrists have always been interested in what people worry about—after all, worries are what most people take with them to the psychiatrist's couch. As early as 1939, Rudolf Pintner and Joseph Lev at Columbia University published a children's worry inventory based on the kinds of things that children of the time worried about—an inventory that contained worry items such as "losing your fountain pen" and "witches"! They summarized the worries they collected into categories, including school, family, economic, personal health and well-being, and social adequacy—all of which are arguably as relevant today as they were in the 1930s.[37]

In 1986 Patricia Wisocki and colleagues at the University of Massachusetts published a worry scale for elderly populations.[38] This had three clear domains—finances, health, and social conditions—all of which resonated with the worries expressed by the children in Pintner and Lev's earlier study, suggesting there may be a good deal of stability across age ranges in the kinds of things we worry about.

In the 1990s, I collaborated with my good friend Frank Tallis, a clinical psychologist (who has since become a best-selling crime novelist), to develop the Worry Domains Questionnaire (WDQ), which was designed to provide objective and measurable details of what people worried about. We asked a large sample of individuals to tell us their main worries and then grouped these worries into semantically similar clusters. This resulted in five domains of worry: relationships ("that I will lose close friends"), lack of confidence ("that I feel insecure"), aimless future ("that I'll never achieve my ambitions"), work ("that I make mistakes at work"), and financial ("that I am not able to afford things").

None of these domains will come as any surprise to those of us who are worriers. They are all central themes of our everyday living and reflect the practicalities of life and our psychological reactions to them. Different groups within society worry more about some domains than others. For instance, students worry more about work items than other domains, reflecting their focus on their academic studies. However, working individuals worry more about financial issues than other domains. What is also interesting is that individuals with a diagnosed anxiety disorder, such as generalized anxiety disorder (GAD) or obsessive-compulsive disorder (OCD), score significantly higher than nonclinical populations on the domains questionnaire, suggesting that individuals with these disorders are still largely worrying about the same kinds of things as healthy individuals—but significantly more so.[39] Exercise 3 in this chapter gives you the opportunity to complete the WDQ and to compare your worrying across various worry topics.

The WDQ along with the studies described above suggest that major worries tend to group around familiar domains that include relationships, finances, work, and health,[40] and these reflect anxieties triggered by things such as love and marital status, loneliness, poverty, unemployment, economic status, and disability. These are worries that are driven by traditional sources of anxiety and, as such, would have been worries experienced by previous generations and even our more ancient ancestors.

Yet, as I outlined in my recent book *The Anxiety Epidemic*, the topics of our main worry may be traditional ones, but within each of these worry topics, our focus has subtly changed and created some new angles on old worries that have developed only in the last few decades.

For example, the financial crisis of 2007–2008 had a devastating impact on employment, with the rate of unemployment in the US rising from 5.8 percent in 2007 to 9.6 percent in 2010, with some studies directly linking this crisis to increased rates of suicide since 2007.[41] Being unemployed is in itself a devastating experience, both financially and in terms of the blows to self-esteem and productivity caused by failing to find work.

It's not just the economic consequences of being unemployed that give rise to worries; the modern-day job search itself creates anxiety, as does the anticipation of rejection, and technology may contribute significantly to the factors that make unemployment and job-seeking an even more stressful and worrying process. For example, new technology forces the job applicant to persistently seek ways of refining their applications, evolve better interview techniques, seek and collate relevant job information, and sadly, wake regularly throughout the night worrying about the next steps in this relentless search for employment. Some employment agencies calculate that nowadays someone seeking work should expect to attend around fourteen interviews before finally being offered the job they'd accept. The modern job seeker's lot is not just the depression associated with the loss of a job, but the anxiety-provoking worry of refining the résumé, cramming for the interviews, and handling the growing volume of rejections.

Finances are also a core topic for our worries, and financial anxieties and worries have shown a significant increase in recent years—at least in part as a consequence of disruption caused by the COVID-19 pandemic.[42] As much as we'd like to be rid of such worries, we still manage to create more subtle forms of worry about our money and our financial status, especially in countries where the gap between rich and poor appears to be widening.[43] One consequence of this income inequality is a relatively new form of worry, known as "status anxiety."

In a report for the GINI (Growing Inequalities Impact) Project, Marii Paskov and colleagues from the University of Amsterdam assessed the effects of income inequalities across a range of European countries.[44] They found that income inequality was associated with higher levels of status-seeking, suggesting that people are more worried about their position in the social and economic hierarchy where income inequalities are high. What is interesting is that these concerns about status and striving to increase status are not just restricted to the poor, but both the poor and the rich feel more anxious about their status in unequal societies. In effect, while worry associated directly with poverty may be on the decrease, "status-anxiety" worry associated with income inequalities is burgeoning across all income groups.

One of the most common worry domains across all age groups is health, and we've known for a long time that chronic illnesses, such as heart disease, stroke, cancer, diabetes, obesity, and arthritis, put people at greater risk of developing anxiety and depression. However, in most developed countries, life expectancy is increasing with the progress made by medical science, so are health worries on the decline? Maybe not, and the reasons are quite subtle. For example, in figures published in the US in 2018, life expectancy in the US increased from 75.5 years in 1990 to 78.9 years in 2016, and death rates at all ages decreased—leading the report to conclude that the United States made substantial progress in improving health.[45] However, the report also noted that "individual states have had limited success in reducing disability"—especially disability resulting from drug-use disorders, depression, and anxiety, all of which increased in prevalence significantly between 1990 and 2016. What is clear from this report is that significant progress has been made in improving health and in improving life expectancy in the US. A major consequence of the fall in mortality rates is that more people are living longer but living longer with chronic illness and disability—and we know that living with disability gives rise to mental distress and worry, which is up to 4.6 times higher than in those without disabilities.[46]

These are just a few examples of the ways in which the nature of our traditional topics of worry can evolve and change as the world around us changes, and now the following exercise will give you the opportunity to identify your own major worry domains.

EXERCISE 3: Measuring Your Worry Domains

Major worries tend to group around familiar domains that include relationships, finances, work, and health,[47] and these reflect anxieties triggered by things such as love and marital status, loneliness, poverty, unemployment, economic status, and disability. These are worries that are driven by traditional sources of anxiety and as such are worries experienced by most people at some time or other in their lives. In this exercise, you have the opportunity to identify your own major worry domains.

Materials

> Pen or pencil

> The Worry Domains Questionnaire

What It Is

In this exercise, you can complete the Worry Domains Questionnaire and take a look at how your worrying compares in different domains of traditional worry topics, such as relationships, work, finances, and self-confidence.

How Will This Help My Worrying?

You'll be able to identify the topics that worry you the most and to see how you compare on these worry domains with norms that are available for other groups of people.

How to Do It

First, complete the Worry Domains Questionnaire below or download it from http://www.newharbinger.com/50348. For each worry thought, rate your worry about it using the following scale:

> 0 = not at all

> 1 = a little

> 2 = moderately

> 3 = quite a bit

> 4 = extremely

Be honest! There are no correct answers.

Worry Domains Questionnaire (WDQ)

Using the above rating scale of 0 to 4, indicate how much you worry about each worry thought below.

_____ I worry that my money will run out. (Finances)

_____ I worry that I cannot be assertive or express my opinions. (Lack of confidence)

_____ I worry that my future job prospects are not good. (Aimless future)

_____ I worry that my family will be angry with me or disapprove of something that I do. (Relationships)

_____ I worry that I'll never achieve my ambitions. (Aimless future)

_____ I worry that I will not keep my workload up to date. (Work incompetence)

_____ I worry that financial problems will restrict vacations and travel. (Finances)

_____ I worry that I have no concentration. (Aimless future)

_____ I worry that I am not able to afford things. (Finances)

_____ I worry that I feel insecure. (Lack of confidence)

_____ I worry that I can't afford to pay my bills. (Finances)

_____ I worry that my living conditions are inadequate. (Finances)

_____ I worry that my life may have no purpose. (Aimless future)

_____ I worry that I don't work hard enough. (Work incompetence)

_____ I worry that others will not approve of me. (Lack of confidence)

_____ I worry that I find it difficult to maintain a stable relationship. (Relationships)

_____ I worry that I leave work unfinished. (Lack of confidence)

_____ I worry that I lack confidence. (Lack of confidence)

_____ I worry that I am unattractive. (Relationships)

_____ I worry that I might make myself look stupid. (Lack of confidence)

_____ I worry that I will lose close friends. (Relationships)

_____ I worry that I haven't achieved much. (Aimless future)

_____ I worry that I am not loved. (Relationships)

_____ I worry that I will be late for an appointment. (Work incompetence)

_____ I worry that I make mistakes at work. (Work incompetence)

Add up the scores for the five items in each domain. So, add up the scores for all five items labeled "relationships," all five items labeled "lack of confidence," all five items labeled "aimless future," all five items labeled "work incompetence", and all five items labeled "financial." Finally, add up all your domain scores to give yourself one single overall score for the questionnaire.

Compare the five scores for the five worry domains. Is one or more domain score significantly higher than the others? If so, can you think of a reason why this might be?

TIPS

- Different samples of people score differently on these five domains. Working people tend to score high on the financial worry domain, while student samples score highest on the work domain, presumably reflecting a focus on their academic activities.

- Where scores are available, studies suggest that the average WDQ total score for a nonclinical individual is between 23 and 27 (regardless of whether the individual is a working person or a student).[48] How does your total score compare with these norms—is it higher or lower? However, remember that these norms were taken from samples more than twenty years ago. Levels of worrying appear to have increased significantly in the last couple of decades among certain groups of individuals, so if your total score is above these norms, you may still be quite average in your level of worrying by current standards.

- Scores on the WDQ for individuals with diagnosable anxiety-based disorders are significantly higher than the scores for nonclinical individuals, with mean scores for individuals with a diagnosis of GAD or OCD usually 40 or higher. If you scored over 40 and you find your worrying distressing, it would be wise to seek help for your worrying from your family practitioner or an accredited counselor or psychotherapist. However, it's important to be aware that a high score on the WDQ does *not necessarily* mean that you have an anxiety-based disorder.

The Hassle of Daily Hassles

WORRY FACT 5. Nowadays we can spend as much of our day worrying about niggly daily hassles as we do about longer-term traditional worry topics.

In 2015, the insurance provider Direct Line published a survey of worries after asking 2,025 adults about the stressors that affected them on a daily basis.[49] Here are the top ten daily worries in rank order: (1) not being able to sleep, (2) losing your keys, (3) being stuck in a traffic jam when already late, (4) losing an important paper or document, (5) having nowhere to park, (6) the printer not working when you need to print something, (7) running out of battery on your mobile phone while out, (8) discovering you're out of toilet paper while you're on the toilet, (9) dealing with computerized customer service, and (10) realizing you've forgotten your bank card when paying for an item.

What's striking about this list is that at least some of these daily hassles would have meant nothing a generation ago because they are related to technologies and twenty-first-century living. Basically, you're not just going to wake up in the middle of the night worrying about longer-term anxieties, like finances, health, and relationships; you're going to wake up worrying about those niggling daily hassles that could blight your day tomorrow— things like parking problems, charging your smartphone, broken printers, and traffic jams. These niggling worries will be as intense and as unsettling as longer-term traditional worries and will still keep you awake at night. And here's the irony: one of the main modern-day worries is not being able to sleep. How did we get ourselves into this perfect vicious cycle?

Professor Jonathan Freeman of Goldsmith's College London has coined the term "fearcasting" to describe this modern-day worrying about daily hassles in which we forward-plan for potential eventualities, such as those listed above. Professor Freeman writes that "we weren't expecting to find that one of the major triggers (for stress and worrying) is the way in which people mentally process the spiraling effects of an everyday emergency...you may have sat in traffic on your way to the train station—and the worry about having to pay for a new ticket after missing the train can cause a feeling of hysteria!"[50] We're not just worrying about future life event scenarios; our lives are so busy that our brain is continuously planning how to deal with a whole range of daily hassles—missed trains, parking problems, dead phones, lost keys, and traffic jams—many of which, of course, may simply never happen. This is classic catastrophizing on a daily basis.

The Curse of Technology and Perpetual Connectivity

WORRY FACT 6. Technological advances, such as the development of the internet, have created many new sources of worry that would not have been experienced by previous generations.

WORRY FACT 7. New modern-day worries include those created by the widespread use of social media and the increased consumption of news that has become 24/7, difficult to avoid, increasingly visual and shocking, and increasingly negative and fear laden.

One of humanity's most influential inventions in recent times has been the internet. But like most influential developments, it has both good and bad sides, and these good and bad sides are reflected in social media. At first glance, social networking sites, such as Facebook, Twitter, and Instagram, seem to be a modern means of facilitating our connectedness with others, sharing activities and news, and keeping in touch with friends both old and new. What could go wrong?

Quite a bit has gone wrong, and social media is arguably responsible in some way for many of the worries we experience in the modern era—especially the worries of young people who are learning about intense, committed relationships for the first time in the context of perpetual connectivity provided by social media. Today, social media, such as Facebook, Twitter, and Instagram, is a significant contributor to the friendship networks of most people, so whether you perceive yourself to be a successful user of social media is likely to influence what you worry about on a daily basis and impact on your feelings of loneliness, anxiety, paranoia, and your mental health generally.

The relatively modern phenomenon of social media and its associated technology adds a new dimension to loneliness, anxiety, and worry by offering the user a way of directly quantifying friendships, viewing the friendship networks of others for comparison, and providing immediate information about social events. You can compare your own popularity with that of your peers and address that fear of missing out (FOMO) by continually monitoring what's going on socially. It's easy to see how internet use can take the place of more traditional social interaction and provide a yardstick for your own popularity—or more significantly, your own feelings of loneliness and alienation.

Interestingly, the recent COVID-19 pandemic has provided all the conditions for a "natural" experiment on the effects of replacing physical social interactions with connectivity via social media, and the internet became a significant means of contact between individuals during the lockdowns of the pandemic period. In spite of social media satisfying the need to socially connect with other human beings, recent studies suggest that during the pandemic, use of social media was inversely related to happiness.[51]

One hypothesis for this relationship is that social networks facilitate unfavorable social comparisons. People tend to post photos and news on social media that show them in a favorable light—and this makes the feeds of your contacts seem like perfect lives, triggering worries in your own mind about how your own life seems so unexciting in comparison.[52] This effect of social media is especially prevalent in young people and especially in individuals who use social media in a passive way—that is, those who follow the posts of others but rarely post themselves. Our use of social media to chase connectedness in this way may merely make us worry more about feeling disconnected and lonelier. If you log on to Facebook every day, like more than half of all Facebook users in the world, and you use it in a passive way, it will merely reinforce your feelings of disconnectedness.

Furthermore, a study of college-student Facebook use by Jay Campisi and colleagues at Regis University in Colorado found that almost all respondents experienced some form of Facebook-induced stress and that this stress was directly associated with physical health problems, such as upper respiratory infections.[53] But what was interesting was that this stress wasn't a function of how small a respondent's social network was, but how large it was—the larger the Facebook social network, the greater the stress and worrying. So a large network of friends on social networking sites appears to be an added source of stress and worry to today's young people.

The added stress and anxiety that large virtual social networks bring has been well illustrated in a study by Julie Morin-Major and colleagues at Harvard.[54] They found that after controlling for other relevant factors such as sex, age, and time of awakening; perceived stress; and perceived social support, the larger your Facebook network, the greater your daytime cortisol production—and higher awakening cortisol levels are associated with chronic stress, worry, and burnout and are a vulnerability factor for depression. The authors of this study speculated that the number of Facebook friends you have might be positive up to a point and offer social reassurance and social support, but after this optimum level is passed, social support may switch to social pressure and lead to increased stress, more worrying, and higher cortisol levels.

Another consequence of technology's perpetual connectivity is the way that the news we consume is presented and how it now provides a stimulus for stress and worry. News reporting changed with the advent of the internet, perpetual connectivity, twenty-four-hour news channels, news alerts, and social media. You can now get access to news 24/7—whether you want it or not. And many of us do not want it, but we still keep those news alerts on our smartphones.

But it's not the perpetual access to news that is necessarily the most significant change in the way news is presented—new technology has allowed its modern-day tone to be increasingly emotive, its medium increasingly visual and shocking, and its commentaries increasingly negative and fear laden.

As Mark Deuze writes in his book *Media Life*, news media are ubiquitous, pervasive, and cannot be switched off in the modern world. Immediate daily information about world events has become an accepted reality of everyday existence. But a more significant impact of the digital age on news reporting has been the dramatic shift to visual imagery in news items—especially visual imagery contributed by the audience and garnered by journalists from social media. User-generated images of important world events are now regularly captured on the smartphones of those close to or even directly involved in these events, and this new form of "news reality" began to appear during the Asian tsunami of 2004, the 7/7 London underground bombings in 2004, and the Boston marathon bombings of 2013—developments that effectively allowed the audience to witness such events in real time.[55]

News has become increasingly visual, with images taken from multiple sources and presented especially to convey fear, danger, excitement, and risk.[56] The news audience is now effectively transported to the site of a news event by real-time images so that those watching become directly connected to the distressing events that are happening and the affect these events generate—"the media does not merely report the scene but is part of the scene and action."[57]

More than half of all Americans now say that the news causes them stress, anxiety, and worry, yet one in ten checks the news at least every hour, and one in five reports constantly monitoring their social media for the most recent headlines.[58] Clearly, whether negative news is sensationalized or emotionalized fact, speculative commentary, or even mere politically motivated fakery or fake news, its psychological impact on anxiety, worrying, and the mental health of consumers is becoming increasingly recognized—an effect that is exacerbated as modern-day news becomes something that is increasingly difficult to avoid.[59]

If you feel overwhelmed by negative news and the worries it creates, try the following exercise to help you manage your news consumption.

EXERCISE 4: Managing Your News Consumption

I described in this chapter how news has become increasingly negative, emotion laden, visual, and most important, increasingly difficult to avoid. Many worriers find their news consumption distressing—especially when it conveys highly visual imagery of negative events, such as conflict, terrorism, divisive politics, famine, and natural disasters. In chapter 1, I described a study on the effects of negative news, and not only did negative news make people feel more anxious and depressed, it also made them more likely to catastrophize their personal worries.[60]

Materials

Pen or pencil

Notebook

Daily news source (if required)

What It Is

In an age in which news consumption has become difficult to control, the following exercise is designed to help you manage your news consumption and avoid some of the worry-generating effects of negative news.

How Will This Help My Worrying?

Because news is available 24/7 on twenty-four-hour news channels, social media, and smartphone alerts, it's difficult to avoid unless you take some specific actions to manage your consumption. It's not just about when and how often you consume news; it's also about what kind of news you consume. In this exercise, I provide a strategy for confining your news consumption to a specific "news time" each day—you'll also find some tips on how to begin managing your access to news in the "Tips" section.

How to Do It

"News time" is a period of time you set aside each day to take in the news. Choose an amount of time for your news time (for example, thirty minutes) and a convenient time of day to hold your news time (for example, in the early evening after work, before you have dinner). Depending on how you take your news, you may want to watch news clips from earlier in the day, read a newspaper, or access relevant websites that provide details of the news you're interested in. Each day only access the news during your designated news time unless you need to access a news item that has specific and important relevance to you (for example, news about flooding in your area).

Here are some important dos and don'ts for news time:

- Don't consume only headlines during your news time. Make sure you're consuming news that puts each news item into context that will stop you speculating about a broad range of potential catastrophic outcomes that are unlikely to ever happen.

- Don't schedule your news time just prior to bedtime when you might end up taking your worries about the news to bed with you.

- Have some mood-lifting strategies available after your news time in case you need them (see exercise 6 in chapter 6).

- If vivid visual images in negative news items cause you distress, then try to use your news time to access the news in nonvisual ways, such as by reading newspapers or listening to the news on a radio channel.

- If you become worried about a news item during the day, write that worry down, take it with you to your news time where you can deal with it there, and perhaps discover more relevant information about it that helps you put it into a less-threatening context.

- If you find a news item threatening or anxiety-provoking, think about how likely it is that the events in the news item might affect you specifically. Remember, the majority of negative news items may make you feel anxious, but the events in those news items are highly unlikely to affect you personally (for example, viewing an item about a murder in a distant city does not mean that you personally are more likely to be harmed).

- Finish your news time when your scheduled time is up and make sure you have a distracting activity available immediately after your news time (such as dinner, a walk around the block, or watching an entertaining show).

TIPS

- Avoid twenty-four-hour news channels—especially dipping in to such channels at irregular times during the day "just to see if anything dramatic is happening." If you access these channels with the intention of discovering dramatic news, then you'll probably find it in some form or other—even if it's only you bringing your negative threat interpretation bias to your viewing!

- If you do take in news headlines, try to explore the broader context in which those events are occurring, for example, by accessing longer-form journalism, in-depth commentaries, or documentaries that provide context that prevents you from over-catastrophizing simplistic and sensationalized headlines.

- Many people nowadays consume news only on social media. But beware, many sources of news on social media may be unreliable, politically motivated, or simply sensationalized fake news or spam. If you're interested in a particular news topic, ask yourself, What's the best and most reliable source of information on this topic? For example, if you're interested in facts about COVID-19, don't rely solely on the information on social media; try looking at summaries provided by the World Health Organization or the US Department of Health and Human Services.

- If you feel that your mood has been negatively affected by the news, you can use one or more of the mood-boosting strategies described in exercise 6 in chapter 6. Because moods are only short-term changes in how you feel, they can be changed relatively effectively using mood-lifting strategies that suit you.

- If you're worried about a particular news item and find it anxiety provoking or distressing, you might want to try to "cognitively downgrade" these worries by taking a look at exercise 13 in chapter 8. The cognitive neutralizing strategies in this exercise provide a variety of statements you can use to try to put the news item you're worrying about into a less anxiety-provoking perspective.

Worry in the Twenty-First Century

The catastrophic worrier can usually worry about any topic in the known universe (and beyond). Whatever that topic, you can make it worse than it seemed at the start of your worrying, invent multiple negative outcomes that will never happen, and beat yourself up in the process. But, as we might expect, worries tend to gravitate around life problems—problems related to health, finances, work, and relationships. We worry about these things, and our ancestors also worried about these things. But for each generation, there's a different twist to these worries, and as society develops, so too do new angles on these traditional worries.

In contrast, each new generation also creates entirely new worries—worries that would be unknown to any previous generation. Today, many of these new worries relate to technologies that form the essential infrastructure of modern-day living. They affect the way we communicate with each other and the way we learn about the world. On their own, none would seem inherently bad. But together they create a web of perpetual connectivity that means you get no respite from incessant streams of information and no respite from the online activities of your friends, from work, or from news of world events. In fact, courtesy of the internet, you also get no respite from the fact that anything you want to know about is available at the click of a mouse button—all grist for the modern-day worry mill.

CHAPTER 4

Worried Sick

How Does Worrying Affect Your Mental and Physical Health?

Roadmap of the chapter. We're all familiar with the phrase "worried sick," but does worry really make you sick? In this chapter, we look at the role that worrying may play in the development of both mental health problems and physical illnesses. I begin by discussing the role that worry plays in the development of mental health problems—and particularly the role pathological worry plays in the development of anxiety disorders, generalized anxiety disorder (GAD), and even insomnia and sleep-related problems. The second half of the chapter investigates whether chronic worrying has a causal effect on your physical health and how it might trigger the physiological stress reactions that are risk factors for cardiovascular illness, somatic complaints, endocrine problems, and opportunistic infections.

Catastrophic worrying is not a good thing, but how much of a bad thing is it? Can chronic catastrophic worrying damage your health? If the commonly used phrase "I'm worried sick!" is anything to go by, we'd expect to find a significant link between worrying and health.

This raises some interesting questions. I hinted earlier that catastrophic worrying is associated with diagnosable mental health problems—but if that is the case, what is the relationship? Do mental health problems promote chronic worrying, or is worrying itself a risk factor for diagnosable mental health conditions?

In a similar vein, what's the relationship between worrying and physical health problems? We know that worrying is a close ally of stress and anxiety, and the latter have been linked to many physical health conditions, including somatic complaints such as pain and headaches, cardiovascular illness, reduced immune system levels, endocrine disorders, and slower recovery from physical illnesses.[61] But does chronic worrying have a direct effect on our physical health, and can we improve our physical health by reducing our worrying? Let's begin by looking at the relationship between worry and mental health problems.

Worrying and Mental Health

WORRY FACT 1. Levels of worrying are significantly higher in anyone diagnosed with an anxiety disorder.

WORRY FACT 2. Catastrophic worrying can lead to the development of irrational fear beliefs that maintain individual anxiety disorders.

WORRY FACT 3. Many people who develop an anxiety disorder combine catastrophic worrying with uncompromising avoidance behavior—a combination that helps to maintain the anxiety disorder over time.

WORRY FACT 4. When a mental health problem is caused by a specific event or experience, continued worry and rumination about that event can maintain the mental health problem long after the precipitating event has passed.

As early as 1992, clinical psychologists Timothy Brown, Martin Antony, and David Barlow investigated the worry levels of 436 anxiety-disorder patients at the University of New York Center for Stress and Anxiety Disorders.[62] They found that patients diagnosed with an anxiety disorder exhibited worry levels significantly higher than healthy control participants, and this included patients diagnosed with anxiety problems, such as panic disorder, social anxiety disorder, specific phobias, obsessive-compulsive disorder, and GAD. Anxiety disorders are not pleasant conditions to experience, and their defining diagnostic criterion is that they cause significant distress and disability to the suffer. And it seems they also come with the added burden of pathological worrying.

This relationship between anxiety disorders and worrying is not surprising given that all anxiety disorders come with an elevated threat bias. In all cases, individuals with an anxiety disorder are anxious because they perceive significant threats and challenges in their lives. These threats may be either real or imagined, but regardless of this status, they still provide the basis for chronic bouts of worrying.

Let's take the uncomplicated example of the person who is spider phobic. Most individuals who are spider phobic are anxious about spiders but rarely anxious about anything else. They've acquired a spider phobia because they've developed specific beliefs about spiders being threatening or dangerous. These beliefs will differ from one spider phobic to another but typically include harm beliefs ("when a spider is near me, it will bite me"), unpredictability beliefs ("when I encounter a spider, it will run in an elusive way"), invasiveness beliefs ("spiders will crawl into my clothes"), and response beliefs ("when I see a spider, I will faint"). These beliefs provide the fodder for regular catastrophic worrying about potential interactions with spiders—interactions that rarely end up in the catastrophic outcomes that this worrying generates. Similarly, individuals with other anxiety disorders also catastrophize their exaggerated threat beliefs, and this process probably accounts for much of the elevated levels of worry in those with anxiety disorders.

This seems to suggest that anxiety disorders cause you to worry, but does worrying cause you to develop an anxiety disorder? There is good reason to believe it does. First, we've already seen in chapter 1 that catastrophic worrying can make you anxious. It generates threatening outcomes by the dozen—all of which are triggers for anxiety and stress—and research has regularly shown that the longer a worry bout continues, the more distressed the catastrophic worrier becomes.[63]

Second, the exaggerated threat beliefs of individuals with anxiety disorders must come from somewhere, and one of the sources for these exaggerated beliefs is catastrophic worrying. If you're continually asking yourself catastrophic "What if…?" questions, you're generating numerous hypothetical threatening or challenging outcomes—and some of them will stick, and they'll stick for a considerable time. The reason for this is that many people adopt the perfect strategy of generating an anxiety disorder by combining catastrophic worrying with uncompromising avoidance behavior—and that's a powerful and pernicious combination! Generate a few hypothetical nasty outcomes and then spend the rest of your time trying to avoid them!

Why is avoidance such a disastrous partner for catastrophic worrying? Catastrophic worrying generates a multitude of threatening outcomes of a worry, and avoidance behavior prevents you from finding out that the threats may not be real. Perfect, don't you think? You couldn't design a better system for generating an anxiety disorder. So, in the case of the spider phobic, catastrophic worrying generates many potential beliefs about fearful outcomes of encountering a spider, but the phobic's avid avoidance of spiders prevents them from being able to disconfirm these beliefs, enabling fear of spiders to be maintained potentially indefinitely. If you believe there's a monster in the closet, but you're too frightened to open the door, then your fear of the closet monster will never be disconfirmed. This is how everyday catastrophic worrying can generate chronic anxiety problems if you combine it with inflexible avoidance behaviors.

All anxiety disorders are underpinned by dysfunctional beliefs about something that the sufferer believes is threatening or fearful, and I've provided some examples of these beliefs in the table below. You can probably work out how catastrophic worrying might allow these kinds of extreme and often irrational beliefs to develop, and these types of exaggerated fear beliefs are the kinds of cognitions that are identified and addressed in cognitive behavior therapy (CBT) for anxiety disorders.

Examples of Exaggerated Fear Beliefs That Occur in the Five Main Types of Anxiety Disorders

Anxiety Disorder	Dysfunctional Fear Beliefs
Specific phobia	*I'll definitely fall and kill myself if I stand on a high balcony.* *When a spider is in my vicinity, it will crawl toward my private parts.*
Social anxiety disorder	*I fear I'll behave in a socially inept way in front of my friends.* *People will evaluate me negatively when I give my presentation.*
Panic disorder	*When my heart starts to beat faster, it means I'm going to have a heart attack and die.* *I must avoid crowded places in case I have a panic attack and collapse in front of people.*
Generalized anxiety disorder (GAD)	*I must meet all my responsibilities all the time; otherwise, I'll be a failure.* *I must always try to eliminate uncertainty in case that leads to bad things happening.*
Obsessive-compulsive disorder (OCD)	*I must never use a public restroom because I will become contaminated and spread disease among my family.* *If I don't complete my elaborate checking ritual to be sure the gas stove is off, there will be an explosion, and someone will die.*

One final fact: When mental health problems are caused by specific traumatic events in an individual's life, catastrophic worrying and rumination can maintain that mental health problem long after the original traumatic cause has passed. For example, Alison Holman and colleagues at the University of California assessed 2,729 adults for acute stress responses following the terrorist attack on the Twin Towers in New York on 9/11 and then followed up these individuals over the following two- to three-year period.[64] They found that many people were still experiencing acute stress responses years later, and interestingly, these were individuals who still had ongoing worries about terrorism. It appeared that their ongoing tendency to worry and ruminate about the events of 9/11 had maintained their stress reaction for many years after the precipitating event. Perhaps most importantly, this continued tendency to worry was also associated with physical health issues, which I'll discuss in more detail later in this chapter.

Generalized Anxiety Disorder (GAD)

WORRY FACT 5. The most significant diagnostic criterion for GAD is worry that is excessive and occurs for more days than not over a minimum of six months.

WORRY FACT 6. GAD is relatively prevalent with a lifetime prevalence rate of 3.7 percent.

WORRY FACT 7. GAD is associated with other stress-related symptoms, such as difficulty concentrating, irritability, muscle tension, and sleep disturbance.

WORRY FACT 8. There is a significant reciprocal relationship between pathological worrying and insomnia.

Arguably the mental health disorder most relevant to catastrophic worrying is GAD, and in chapter 2, I introduced you to Jim, a fifty-four-year-old man who had been diagnosed with GAD after a series of negative life events left him unable to shake off his perpetual worrying, which he felt was "driving him mad."

DSM-5, the most influential mental health diagnostic manual, specifies a number of criteria for a diagnosis of GAD. The most significant of these criteria are worry-based. For example, worry must be excessive and occur for more days than not over a minimum of six months; worry must be related to a range of events or topics and not just restricted to, say, one individual worry; and worry must feel uncontrollable and cause significant distress or impairment of social, occupational, or family functioning.[65] In relative terms, GAD is quite a prevalent problem: 3.7 percent of the population will be diagnosed with GAD in their lifetime,[66] and up to 12 percent of the population will experience disabling and distressing subclinical symptoms (symptoms that are distressing but just fail to meet the criteria for a diagnosis) in their lifetime.[67] In the US, that equates to almost forty million people suffering the disabling and distressing symptoms of pathological worrying at some point in their life.

But we should be clear that GAD is not just a disorder of worrying; it's associated with other stress-related symptoms, which are necessary for the diagnosis, and these include feeling continuously on edge, difficulty concentrating, irritability, muscle tension, and perhaps most importantly, sleep disturbance. To be sure, many of these more physical symptoms may in fact be consequences of uncontrollable worrying—especially the tension and edginess and the restlessness and insomnia. These symptoms are perhaps less surprising if we acknowledge that individuals with GAD spend much of their time maintaining a tense alertness in readiness to worry about potential future threats and challenges (see chapter 5).

However, it's only recently that clinicians have become concerned about the significant relationship between worry and insomnia. To use a corny metaphor, GAD and insomnia are regular bedfellows. Up to 90 percent of GAD sufferers report dissatisfaction with their sleep, and up to 68 percent can be classified as having either moderate or severe insomnia. GAD sufferers exhibit increased wake time at night as well as decreased sleep efficiency and total sleep time. Research suggests that worry and insomnia often occur together to form a reciprocal relationship in which each one negatively affects the other. In Germany, Carolin Thielsch and colleagues at the University of Münster tracked the behavior of fifty-six individuals who had a diagnosis of GAD.[68] These individuals carried a portable device for one week and logged sleep quality and worry processes four times a day. They found that reduced sleep quality at night was followed by increased levels of worrying when awaking the next morning and during the subsequent day. The opposite relationship was also found: worry assessed directly before going to bed predicted subsequent poor sleep quality.

Most of you who've experienced chronic worry will not be at all surprised by the results of this research. We've all had a rotten night's sleep after a day of stressful worrying and a debilitating day worrying about everything after a lousy sleepless night. But this process can become endemic for the GAD sufferer, and this has two particular consequences.

First, insomnia and poor-quality sleep are not just causes of further worrying; insomnia is now considered to be a significant risk factor for a whole range of mental health problems, including anxiety, depression, bipolar disorder, post-traumatic stress disorder, substance use disorders, and suicide.[69] This suggests that treating insomnia and its causes would be a useful preventative mental health strategy.

Second, many contemporary treatments now recommend that an intervention for insomnia be concurrently included with treatment for GAD symptoms. For these reasons, I've included an exercise in this chapter on managing your worry at night as well as some tips drawn from contemporary CBT treatments of insomnia—tips that can help you manage insomnia and develop more healthy sleeping patterns.

EXERCISE 5: Managing Your Worry at Night

Nighttime is the time when people tend to worry most. If your worry prevents you sleeping at night, try this exercise. It's best to begin managing your worry during the day first, perhaps by drawing up a worry worksheet and scheduling daily worry time (see exercise 12 in chapter 8). Once you've achieved this, you can try taking your Worry Time Worksheet to bed with you and "letting go" of the worries that trouble you at night by writing them in the worksheet and saving them for tomorrow's worry time. Finally, if you think you may need them, you can use mindfulness exercises to help you back to sleep (see exercise 16 in chapter 10).

Materials

Pen or pencil

Notebook

Worry Time Worksheet (available for download at http://www.newhar binger.com/50348)

What It Is

If you're a chronic worrier, you are very aware that worrying is particularly common at night and will often prevent you getting to sleep or staying asleep. This exercise is designed to help you manage your worries at night and to find a few ways of getting to sleep when your worries have kept you awake.

How Will This Help My Worrying?

In this exercise, we're trying to get you to postpone your worries when they trouble you at night so you can deal with them at a more appropriate time, such as during your daily scheduled worry time.

How to Do It

When you go to bed, take a copy of your Worry Time Worksheet with you, and write down any worries that bother you during the night as they occur.

Writing down the worry and postponing it until the next day will often help you "let go" of the worry. By doing this, you're not ignoring the worry, just ensuring that you can consider the worry properly at a more appropriate time. The worry is written down on your worksheet, so you won't forget it!

If you're having difficulty getting back to sleep at night, try some of the following: (a) focus on the current moment by putting your attention on your breathing, your toes, or the touch of the pillow; (b) try some mindfulness tips, which you can find in exercise 16 in chapter 10; (c) prevent any sleep-monitoring activities by turning the clock away from you so you don't keep looking at the time and try not to keep thinking about whether you feel tired or fatigued; and (d) if you've been awake for more than fifteen to twenty minutes, get out of bed, go to another room, try some mindfulness exercises, and don't go back to bed again until you begin to feel relaxed or sleepy.

TIPS

Very often we develop sleep problems because we've gotten into some bad habits that confuse our body and our brain and prevent us from sleeping. Here are a few tips for managing issues related to sleeping, summarized from recent CBT-based insomnia treatments[70]:

- Go to bed only when you feel sleepy. Try not to go to bed when you're still wide awake.

- Don't drink caffeinated drinks in the hours before going to bed.

- Get up each morning at roughly the same time regardless of how much sleep you've had. This will get your body into a regular sleep routine.

- Don't use the bedroom for activities that may conflict with sleep, such as reading, watching TV, eating, sending texts, or searching the internet. Your bedroom surroundings will come to trigger thoughts about these sleep-preventing activities and stop you sleeping (sex is okay though!).

- Don't cancel your appointments the day after a bad night's sleep. This will only make you feel guilty and more anxious and unable to sleep well in the future. In contrast, fulfilling your appointments the next day will often increase your energy levels and make you feel able to cope.

- Many people suffering from insomnia tend to overestimate how long it takes them to get to sleep and underestimate how long they've slept, and these beliefs can maintain their anxieties about not sleeping. To counteract any misbeliefs, complete a sleep diary every morning immediately on waking. Record how long it took you to fall asleep, roughly how much time you were awake at night, and as a result the total amount of time you were asleep. You'll probably discover that you've actually been sleeping for longer than you imagined.

Worry and Physical Health

WORRY FACT 9. There is a strong relationship between worrying and stressful daily hassles that can compromise the immune system.

WORRY FACT 10. Worrying increases the amount of time that stress has a "wear and tear" effect on the human body.

WORRY FACT 11. Worrying about a stressor prolongs the effect of that stressor long after it has passed and, as a consequence, prolongs the physiological stress response that causes damage to cardiovascular and endocrine activity.

Not surprisingly, there is a link between chronic worrying and mental health, but what about worry and physical health? As I mentioned earlier, there's plenty of evidence for a link between anxiety, stress, and physical health. This link occurs at several levels, where stress can adversely affect immune system function, resulting in a greater risk of illness, opportunistic infections, such as colds and flu, and slow recovery from illness and disease. Stress is also implicated in greater risk for somatic complaints (such as aches, pains, and headaches), cardiovascular disease, and pain perception, and although there's still no strong evidence that stress can directly cause cancer, there is growing evidence that stress may be related to a return of cancer after successful treatment due to stress hormones reactivating dormant cancer cells.[71]

There's strong evidence linking worry with stress and physical illness, particularly given that there is a strong relationship between stress and worrying. For example, in chapter 3, I pointed out that much of our modern-day worrying involves catastrophizing minor stressors known as "daily hassles." These are defined as the irritating, frustrating, distressing demands that characterize everyday transactions with the environment, and examples include losing things, traffic jams, bad weather, arguments, and disappointments (and lack of sleep!).[72]

In a study of the relationship between daily hassles and common cold symptoms, psychologist Arthur Stone and colleagues found that the reporting of daily hassles increased in frequency three to four days before the onset of common cold symptoms.[73] They concluded that the stress of daily hassles may well have precipitated common cold symptoms by compromising immune system levels—a finding that has since been replicated in several other studies.

Where does worrying fit into all of this? First, a study we conducted several years ago showed that there is a very strong correlation between daily hassles and frequency of worrying—something we might expect given that most worriers often worry either about the effects of daily hassles or having to encounter future daily hassles.[74] This suggests a close relationship between stress, daily hassles, and worrying but doesn't necessarily indicate that worry itself directly affects processes that may be detrimental to our health. For example, the effects of worrying may be indirect. Worrying may increase our perception of the severity of daily hassles, and that can trigger stress, which in turn releases stress hormones, such as cortisol. This will compromise our immune system if cortisol is released over long periods of time as a result of chronic stress.

Second, we know that worrying usually takes place during periods of negative mood, and there is abundant evidence showing that negative mood results in a lowered immune response to disease and infection.[75] So, worrying may be part of a complex system involving stress and negative affect that compromises immune function and results in physical health problems. Whichever way we try to unravel all these relationships, worry is always in there as one of the culprits—even if at this point, we can only show it guilt by association.

However, Bart Verkuil and Jos Brosschot at Leiden University in the Netherlands and Julian Thayer at Ohio State University have gone one step further and implicated worry directly in the process by which stress causes physical health problems. They argue that worrying increases the total amount of time that stress has a "wear and tear" effect on the human body, and worry does this quite simply by prolonging the amount of time that you consider a stressor to be stressful.[76] That effectively increases the amount of time that you're pumping stress hormones, such as cortisol, into your system and damaging your immune responses.

There are a couple of other examples of how chronic worrying may directly influence physical health. First, Laura Kubzansky and colleagues at the Harvard School of Public Health looked at the relationship between worry and coronary heart disease in a cohort of 1,759 older men between 1975 and 1995.[77] They found that a high level of worrying at the outset of the study was a significant predictor of coronary heart disease during that twenty-year period and concluded that chronic worry may directly increase the risk of coronary problems. Similar findings came from the study I mentioned earlier by Alison Holman and colleagues in which they studied the effects of acute stress caused by the 9/11 terrorist attacks. They found that ongoing worries about terrorism predicted cardiovascular health problems up to two to three years after the original attacks.

Verkuil, Brosschot, and Thayer attributed these findings to the fact that perseverative worrying prolongs the potency of a stressor. So, in the case of the 9/11 study, worries about terrorism ensured that the stressful effects of 9/11 continued way beyond that date, putting extended strain on an individual's immune system and physical health. Taken to its extreme, this view suggests that actually occurring stressors are far less important than what happens subsequently in people's thoughts. That is, their worrying or rumination about the stressor leads to prolonged physiological stress responses that cause most of the damage to physical health, especially in relation to cardiovascular and endocrine activity.[78]

This view is becoming more and more mainstream as accumulating evidence suggests that perseverative negative cognition, such as catastrophic worrying, has a direct effect on somatic health, affecting cardiovascular, autonomic, and endocrine nervous system activity, leading to disease and ill health. It seems you can indeed be "worried sick".[79]

One implication of this apparent direct role that chronic worry has on physical health is that we should be able to ameliorate the effects of stressors by providing interventions for catastrophic worrying following stressful life experiences. Such interventions would limit the long-term physical health effects of the stressor by preventing chronic worrying from maintaining the cognitive potency of the stressor over time. These interventions for pathological worrying would be relevant following common lifetime stressors, such as bereavement, severe illness or medical problems, relationship crises, financial problems, and unemployment, or as part of a rapid crisis-intervention package following life-threatening traumas of the kind that may trigger post-traumatic stress (PTSD) or acute stress symptoms.

Worry Really Can Make You Sick

In this chapter, I described some of the more serious effects of chronic catastrophic worrying. We always knew that there were links of some kind between pathological worrying and mental and physical health problems, but when we dig down and look closely at the evidence, we can see that in many cases, this link between worrying and mental and physical health problems is significant. Pathological worrying is not just a correlate of these problems; there are clear pathways by which worrying can directly influence the development of mental health disorders and physical health conditions.

First, catastrophic worrying can help generate the fear beliefs that maintain all of the main anxiety disorders, and worrying is found at significantly higher levels in many other mental health problems other than anxiety-based ones.

Second, catastrophic worrying maintains the stressful status of a stressor long after that stressor has passed. It acts to keep the stressor "alive" at the cognitive level through generating potential fearful or stressful consequences that the individual believes the stressor may still exert. In turn, these cognitive effects trigger the physiological stress reactions that are risk factors for cardiovascular illness, somatic complaints, endocrine problems, and opportunistic infections. Pathological worrying isn't just an uncomfortable activity that goes on in your head; its negative effects can resonate throughout your whole body.

PART II

WHY YOU WORRY, AND HOW TO STOP

CHAPTER 5

Why Do We Worry About Things That Don't Happen?

Worrying as a Compulsive Lifestyle Choice

Roadmap of the chapter. Much of what we worry about doesn't happen anyway. So why do many of us worry so much? In this chapter, I describe what makes worrying a compulsion that chronic worriers find hard to shake off.

If you're a catastrophic worrier, then you know that worrying takes up a lot of your time. It can prevent you from doing many things that you want to do while you procrastinate over an endless stream of "What if...?" questions. It can make the future seem like a hostile and frightening place. In this chapter, we take an in-depth look at how much of our worrying is worth the effort and then attempt to answer the real conundrum of why we worry so much if most of it is not worth the effort—especially if nine out of every ten worries never actually happen! I'll describe three processes that can turn our worrying into a compulsion: (1) the role of superstitious reinforcement, (2) worrying to prevent even more distressing worries from entering consciousness, and (3) the role of beliefs about the benefits of worrying.

Why Worry? The Role of Superstitious Reinforcement

WORRY FACT 1. A majority of the problems and issues we worry about never actually happen, and some accounts suggest that over 90 percent of what we worry about falls into this category.

WORRY FACT 2. The act of worrying may often be reinforced by the relief experienced when the anticipated threat does not happen.

Let's begin with a bit of French philosophy. In the sixteenth century, Michel de Montaigne was one of the most significant philosophers of the French Renaissance, writing numerous essays that regularly digressed into personal anecdotes and aphorisms. He is best known for his skeptical remark, "Que sais-je?" *What do I know?* But more profound was his later observation: "My life has been filled with terrible misfortune—most of which has never happened!" At first glance, that might seem like a complete contradiction—but in hindsight, it's a perfect description of the catastrophic worrier, someone who is consumed by anxiety by what the future might hold, only to find out eventually that many of those anxieties are unfounded.

You know the experience: Our partner hasn't returned home from work at their usual time, so something must be wrong. *Were they in an accident?*

Maybe they're in the hospital? They're not answering their phone. Perhaps I should call the hospitals just in case. The car did have a faulty tire. What if that caused a blowout on the freeway? Your mind is just about to turn to who will look after the dogs if you have to stay the night at the hospital, when in walks your partner. "I thought I'd stop by the store and get something special for dinner tonight. Oh, and sorry I didn't call; my phone's completely dead!" Your relief is palpable, but you still chastise them for being late! Make a note of the contrasting sentiments in that last sentence—they're more important than you might think.

If you Google the question, "What percentage of what we worry about *never* happens?" you'll regularly find the figure 85 percent. This figure was apparently arrived at by asking people to write down their worries over a period of time and then go back and see which of those worries did and did not happen.[80] The details of the original study are elusive, so it's difficult to check its validity, but that figure is certainly believable.

In fact, research completed in 2020 by Michelle Newman and colleagues at Penn State University suggests that the Google figure of 85 percent is even an underestimate! This study asked chronic high worriers to keep a worry diary and found that on average 91 percent of their worry predictions did not come true. For very many participants, every single one of the worries they recorded failed to happen.[81] The "What if…?" questioning style of catastrophic worriers lends itself perfectly to creating many future scenarios that may feel quite real in the confinements of your mind, but fail to materialize in the living reality of the outside world.

If so much of what the worrier worries about fails to happen, then why worry so much? Is it worth it? Well, it certainly doesn't seem to stop the worrier worrying. The answer may lie partly in the sequence of mental and emotional events that accompany worrying. Just look back at the earlier scenario I described when your partner failed to come home on time. Your worries very quickly involved your partner in an accident and then hospitalized. Your mind then moved on to consider the details of what you'd need to do to stay overnight in the hospital with your badly injured partner. But it's what happens at the end of all this that is most telling.

Two contrasting emotions are released. First, overwhelming relief that your partner is safe. Second, that initial feeling of relief is soon overtaken by an overwhelming desire to chastise those responsible for creating your worry in the first place—the worrier is very likely to insist that their partner always let them know when they'll be late home in the future because… "You know very well I'm a born worrier."

When a supposed worry fails to materialize, relief is significant and may reward the process of worrying. Let me explain this with an anecdote. Another worry researcher and an old friend, Adrian Wells, is professor of clinical psychology at the University of Manchester in England. He has been a significant contributor to our knowledge of pathological worrying and would regularly begin his conference presentations with a dramatic opening statement: "I wake up every morning worrying about being trampled to death by a herd of elephants." The audience would look bemused. A herd of elephants? In Manchester? After a brief pause, he would explain, "But I haven't been trampled to death yet. So my worrying must be working!" This is a rather extreme example but makes a good point. If you view your worrying as a means of trying to ensure that bad things don't happen, then when they don't happen, it may seem as though your worrying has been worth it. There are two factors at work here.

First, the feeling of relief experienced when you realize the worry is unfounded will reinforce whatever went before. This is a form of conditioning in which your worrying is rewarded by the subsequent euphoria you feel when the anxiety is lifted.[82] This causes the release of the neurotransmitter dopamine in the nucleus accumbens—the brain's pleasure center—and causes the activity that precedes the euphoria to be more likely to occur in the future. In this case, that activity is worrying. This is very much like a form of what is known as "superstitious reinforcement."

The classic study of superstitious reinforcement was carried out over fifty years ago by the famous behaviorist B. F. Skinner. He put a hungry pigeon into a box and gave it food every sixty seconds. After being in the box for half an hour, he discovered that the pigeon was exhibiting very stereotyped behavior, such as turning around in a circle and then pecking one of the walls. He called this "superstitious reinforcement" because it appeared the pigeons had begun to repeat the behavior that they were coincidentally performing when food was delivered. They had come to associate a behavior they were performing when food was delivered with food, even though there was no contingent relationship between that behavior and food delivery. In the same way, your worrisome thinking is reinforced because it regularly occurs prior to the relief of the predicted worry not happening—even though the worrying almost certainly has nothing to do with the bad thing failing to happen.

Second, the regular co-occurrence of your worrying with the failure of that worry to actually happen is likely to lead you to develop sets of beliefs about the usefulness of worrying—in particular, that worry is a valuable thing to do to ensure that bad things don't happen. You may not be consciously aware of these beliefs because they develop very slowly over time, but studies suggest that catastrophic worriers do hold these beliefs,[83] and they may develop at least in part from the fact that many of the bad scenarios we create with our worrisome thoughts don't actually happen. I'll talk a little more about these beliefs later.

Does Worrying Protect Us from More Serious Worries?

WORRY FACT 3. Worrying can serve functions other than the identification and solving of problems, and it is these other functions that may maintain chronic levels of worrying. Possibilities include preventing the processing of stressful or aversive images and memories, and a state of worried alertness in order to deal with unexpected threats.

Does worrying become so established because it has a number of different hidden purposes—purposes that are different from simply helping us identify and solve future problems? This is what some researchers have proposed.

There is one particular perplexing fact about people who worry so much that they are diagnosable with a serious anxiety disorder, such as generalized anxiety disorder (GAD; see chapter 4 for further discussion of this condition). We would intuitively expect such people to have high heart rate variability because their constant expectations of fearful or threatening future scenarios would constantly trigger activation of the sympathetic nervous system. Heart rate variability is the rate at which your heartbeats switch from being slow to fast or fast to slow very quickly. But contrary to this expectation, such people have very low heart rate variability and high muscle tension.[84] Psychologist Tom Borkovec and colleagues at Penn State University have argued that this very low heart rate variability is due to a physiological state of "freezing," which is one of the basic fight-fright-flight responses of animals confronted with a threat. It is constant worrying that causes this physiological state and keeps the worrier in a constant state of tension that prevents heart rate from varying much at all.

The argument here is that constant worrying causes this autonomic inflexibility and inhibition of sympathetic nervous system activation by preventing the emotional processing of threatening or frightening images. Worrying is basically a verbal or narrative activity—when we worry, we worry in words, we talk to ourselves about our problems, and researchers, such as Professor Borkovec, argue that this constant stream of internal verbalizations prevents aversive or fearful images entering consciousness.[85] There is something very Freudian about this explanation, where one pathological activity (worrying) is used to repress another pathological activity (processing images and memories that would also be distressing). In lay terms, worrying about imagined dangers also protects us from considering real dangers. If worrying is used to prevent the processing of distressing imagery, we can see that it would be maintained as an activity regardless of whether what we were worrying about was real or not. In fact, if its purpose is to prevent stressful and aversive images entering consciousness, then many of us would see that as good reason to keep on worrying for as long as we can keep it up.

Michelle Newman, also at Penn State University, has a slightly different view of what causes this low heart rate variability in chronic worriers. She argues that low heart rate variability is caused by the fact that catastrophic worriers are highly anxious people who constantly feel vulnerable to unexpected threatening and challenging events. Instead of worrying to prevent the processing of aversive memories and images, Professor Newman claims that many anxious people worry chronically in order to maintain an emotional state that makes them constantly alert to any unexpected threats, and it's this constant alert emotional state that causes a relatively high heart rate with low heart rate variability and high muscle tension.[86]

The anxious catastrophic worrier always wants to be in a state ready to deal with any unexpected threats and will slip automatically into worry mode on the slightest detection of anything that might be threatening or challenging. One interpretation of this view is that this alert worry state serves a survival function for the individual, which will help them deal with any unexpected threats, but in the process, will also automatically trigger much unnecessary worrying to threats that turn out to be imagined and unlikely to happen.

Both of these accounts argue that worrying may occur for purposes other than simply identifying and solving problems, and that is one reason we may end up catastrophically worrying so much about things that are unlikely to happen. According to these accounts, it's not *what* you're worrying about that's important; it's just the fact that you *are* worrying that's important! Does that sound like you? Do you get anxious when you're not worrying and immediately find yourself searching for something to fret about?

The Power of Belief—Worrying as a Lifestyle

WORRY FACT 4. Catastrophic worriers tend to develop strong beliefs that worrying is an important and necessary thing to do to prevent bad things happening.

WORRY FACT 5. Some catastrophic worriers develop strong positive beliefs about the utility of worrying and strong negative beliefs that worrying will also have negative consequences. Such individuals are highly vulnerable to common mental health problems, such as anxiety and depression.

On many occasions throughout this book, you'll come across the phrase frequently uttered by chronic worriers, "I'm a born worrier." On just as many occasions, I have and will continue to argue that worriers are not born that way, but they develop into worriers throughout their lifetime (in ways described in chapter 2). So why are worriers so keen to make everyone believe that they're "born worriers"?

My mother has always been an anxious catastrophic worrier. If worrying were an Olympic sport, she'd already have a cabinet full of gold medals. And while family members regularly attempt to reassure her that the bad things she worries about will actually be fine, she responds with, "You know me, I'm a born worrier." That phrase defines many people—including my mother—and it's a retort that tells us a number of things. It tells us she'll be expecting to worry about something again in the very near future regardless of what we say, and it implies that it's something in her genes that she can't change.

But there is no gene for worrying. It's an activity that's developed over a lengthy period of time by a variety of complex factors that we're going to unpack in this chapter. The complexity of the factors that contribute to chronic worrying makes it very difficult for the worrier to understand why they worry so much—so it seems uncontrollable. An inability to understand why you worry and an inability to control it give rise to the only credible explanation you can think of, which is "I must have been born this way." But as I'll point out many times in this book, that type of reasoning is largely fallacious.

I want to focus now on one particular aspect of your tenacity when it comes to defending your worrying and providing justification for future worrying—the implicit beliefs you are likely to hold about the worry process.

For reasons that are still a little unclear, catastrophic worriers come to believe that worry is a very useful and important thing to do—especially when it comes to avoiding bad things happening. At least in part, these positive beliefs about worry may emerge from some of the processes we've talked about in the previous section. For example, because many worries simply do not materialize, this may make it look as though the worrying was successful, and the sense of relief felt helps develop a belief that, yes, maybe worrying is a good thing to do.

In studies we've conducted, when questioned about their worrying, it becomes clear that catastrophic worriers hold some very strong positive beliefs about how useful worrying is.[87] These can be classed into two groups: (1) worrying motivates me ("In order to get something done, I have to worry about it") and (2) worry helps analytical thinking ("Worrying makes me reflect on life by asking questions I might not usually ask when happy"). These beliefs may seem laudable and like sensible ways to approach life problems, but there is something odd lurking in the background.

First, in these same studies, we found that the more that a worrier holds these positive beliefs, the more likely they are to score on some important measures of psychopathology, including anxiety, depression, pathological worrying, and emotion-focused coping (a form of coping where someone tries to resolve a stressful situation by managing the emotions associated with the situation rather than changing the situation itself). Second, another odd finding was that many worriers simultaneously held both strong beliefs about the positive value of worrying *and* strong beliefs that worrying also had negative consequences. These negative beliefs included (1) "worrying disrupts effective performance," (2) "worrying exaggerates problems," and (3) "worrying causes emotional discomfort."

Imagine the conflict here. Such individuals are driven to worry by the positive beliefs yet are well aware that their worrying causes distress and grief. Indeed, individuals who strongly held both positive and negative beliefs about worrying were the most vulnerable to mental health problems, such as anxiety and depression. They are conflicted by opposing beliefs:

they believe that worrying is something they must do to prevent bad things happening, but they also know that worrying exaggerates their problems and makes them distressed.

However, holding strong positive beliefs about the usefulness of worrying may not automatically be constructive or provide help problem solving—especially if many of these beliefs are superstitious. For example, many of the positive beliefs that worriers endorse are that the act of worrying will in itself make things better ("Worrying allows me to work through the worst that can happen, so when it doesn't happen, things are better"). Also, some positive beliefs require the individual to worry even when things are okay—purely so they might anticipate future negative events ("Worrying makes me reflect on life by asking questions I might not usually ask when happy"). This all paints a picture of the worrier whose positive beliefs about worry are not necessarily contributing to actively solving problems when required, but who is creating a lifestyle in which worrying is the central feature come rain or shine!

The obvious question is: Where do these positive beliefs about worry come from? Many are maladaptive in that they encourage the need to worry even when there's nothing to worry about, making worry a compulsion rather than a discretionary problem-solving tool. The origins of these beliefs may reside in childhood developmental experiences (see chapter 2) or simply in the fact that much of what we worry about doesn't happen—superstitiously reinforcing our beliefs that worrying is a causal factor in generating these happy endings. However, the nice thing about identifying beliefs is that we can become aware of our beliefs—and then manage them and maybe even change them to more functional beliefs.

It seems that catastrophic worriers have somehow created a rod for their own back. The worrier believes that all their worrying is necessary, but it often involves searching for problems that don't exist or attempting to deal with issues that they have no control over. This is a feature of catastrophic worrying that I will try to help you to manage with some tips and advice later in this book.

Reining in the Worry Compulsion

WORRY FACT 6. Catastrophic worriers regularly worry about events and situations they cannot easily influence or change. These include events in the past or events and situations that are highly likely to be determined by the actions of others.

WORRY FACT 7. Worriers usually like to reduce the risk of a worry event happening to zero. This is known as "intolerance of uncertainty," and the inability of worriers to reduce the risk of the bad thing happening to zero is usually a source of distress and anxiety.

If you believe worry is a necessary thing to do—as is the case with most chronic worriers—it is likely to become a catastrophic compulsion. If this is so, then you'll probably spend time looking for things to worry about to satisfy this compulsion. Like the compulsive gambler seeking out opportunities to bet, the compulsive worrier can create a potential threat out of nothing—just to satisfy that urge to worry. This is when worrying becomes a compulsion rather than a matter of choice.

Chronic worrying is a time-consuming and often distressing activity in itself, but if it is also a compulsion, then it causes many other problems as well, because your worry will be entirely indiscriminate about the kinds of worries it'll force you to ruminate about. If there are no important solvable problems around, then the urge to worry will seek out smaller prey and turn them into monsters. It'll turn molehills into mountains and create hypothetical worries that have your brain running around in circles trying to find ways to resolve the unresolvable.

The catastrophic worrier will have conjured up a wide variety of worries to worry about, and one of the first tasks when attempting to manage this feast of anxieties is to begin to categorize your worries into three types: (1) those that are truly not important, (2) those that are important and can be solved, and (3) those that are important but cannot easily be solved.

It's important to take a measured view of your worries and to list them according to those three categories (see also chapter 8). There are some worriers who believe they can control everything by worrying and others who believe they can control nothing, so worry as a consequence. Both of these extremes are unhelpful, which is why you can get some healthy perspective on your problems by listing your worries and sorting them into more practical categories.

Before you start looking closely at each of your worries to see if they can be solved or not, there are some clear types of worry that, by their very nature, will not be easily resolvable. An obvious example is hypothetical "What if...?" worries. These are things that haven't happened yet, but you're anxious that they might. For example, your daughter regularly goes to bars to socialize with her friends, and you're worried she might develop a drinking problem and maybe lose her job as a result. There are two assessments required here: (1) What is the risk? "How likely is it that my daughter will develop a drinking problem?" and (2) How much is determined by the actions of others? "To what extent can I resolve this worry?"

Most worriers don't make risk assessments, but when they do, those assessments deviate from objective reality to some significant degree. Just look back at the guy who catastrophized "getting good grades in school" in chapter 1. Most people would agree that his estimates of bad things happening to him were grossly inflated. But it's not the actual risk of the bad thing happening that is so important to the worrier. It's that they want that risk to be zero, and they want their worrying to help them to reduce that risk to zero. This is known as "intolerance of uncertainty" and is a common feature of chronic worriers. These are people who find any kind of uncertainty aversive, and so there is a continual drive to eradicate uncertainty surrounding life problems. But as my grandmother regularly used to tell me, "There's only one thing in life that's certain...and that's uncertainty!" So continually trying to reduce the risk of any particular bad thing happening to zero is entirely impractical.

But many worriers still deploy sweeping strategies designed to reduce the risk of the bad thing happening to zero if they possibly can, and these inevitably involve attempting to influence the actions of others. Imploring the daughter who socializes in bars to give up alcohol is one risk-eliminating strategy—perhaps with a little emotional blackmail thrown in: "You know how much I'll worry if you keep going to bars and drinking." But there is a point to be made with this example. Worrying drives the worrier to try to control others, and this can damage relationships. But we shouldn't just view this as the catastrophic worrier being a manipulative individual because hypothetical worries, like the one in our example above, will be a genuine source of distress if they go unresolved.

However, there are other solutions to this conundrum that don't require the worrier reducing the risk to zero, and these solutions revolve around helping the worrier to "let go" of hypothetical worries that they cannot resolve easily themselves (help on this is provided in chapter 8).

Apart from "What if…?" hypothetical worries, there are a few other categories of worry that are potentially unresolvable. Common unresolvable worries include worries about the past and worries about what other people are thinking. It's no good worrying about having been a bad parent or having given an embarrassing speech at your best friend's wedding. Both are in the past and cannot be changed, even by the most persistent worrier. You can use these kinds of experiences to inform your present and your future, but it's not productive to agonize over them. Similarly, you can change other people's minds about things, but you will probably have to do it with logic, reasoning, facts, and tact, not by just wishing their minds would change or simply point-blank asking them to change their mind.

Why Do We Worry About Things That Don't Happen?

For many people, worrying can become a compulsion. In this case, it's not so much what you worry about that's important. It's simply worrying per se that's important—even if your worries are not things you can solve or are unlikely to happen. Think carefully about recent occasions when you have been worrying. Could you control your worrying, or did you feel compelled to worry even though the topic of your worry might have been a relatively trivial one?

There are a number of ways in which worrying might become an uncontrollable compulsion, so see if you recognize any of these processes in yourself: (1) worrying might be superstitiously reinforced because of the relief you feel when your worries usually do not happen, (2) the actual act of worrying may prevent more distressing images and thoughts entering your consciousness and so act as a means of repressing even more stressful thoughts and images, or (3) you may have developed very strongly held beliefs that worry is a necessary thing to do—especially if many of the things you worry about do not happen (you believe that worrying may in some way "prevent" bad things happening). Some or all of these processes may contribute to making your worrying a compulsive activity.

CHAPTER 6

The Toxic Duo: Anxiety and Worry

The Collision That Creates Catastrophizing

Roadmap of the chapter. Are worry and anxiety the same thing? Well, no, they're not, and this has some important consequences for catastrophic worrying. In chapter 5, I explained how worry itself can become a compulsive activity—but what happens when we put compulsive worry and anxiety together? This chapter describes how worry and anxiety are different and how anxiety can derail any attempts to adaptively problem solve when we worry. The chapter ends with some tips on how to deal with anxious moods and manage your anxiety when it becomes a chronic condition that disrupts effective worrying.

When I began looking into the nature of worrying decades ago, I was an experimental psychologist, and worrying was very much a legitimate subject of study for someone like me. Worrying is a cognitive activity, and one that we were all aware caused mental distress to a lot of people. So I was impatient to get researching! But then frustration materialized, and to my great surprise, that initial excitement was quickly quashed.

I'd begun by searching the scientific literature for existing research papers on worrying. I can't remember the exact number I found, but it was certainly in the single digits, and two were vague psychoanalytic theses on the possible psychosexual origins of worry—not my cup of tea! This was 1990—the year we launched the Hubble Space Telescope, reunified Germany, and began the Human Genome Project—yet we knew next to nothing about one of the most common cognitive activities of the human mind.

The problem was that, up to that time, most psychologists had simply assumed that anxiety and worrying were the same thing—hardly anyone was studying worrying because they were all studying anxiety and assuming it was identical to worry. But one of the keys to understanding the nature of catastrophic worrying is to recognize that worry and anxiety are simply not the same thing. In fact, worry and anxiety clash like a couple of titans on steroids—toxic twins that collide to create catastrophizing, distress, and cognitive carnage in general. So, let's look at the differences between worry and anxiety and how they interact to cause chronic and pathological worrying. But first let's explore the nature of anxiety.

What Is Anxiety?

WORRY FACT 1. Prior to 1990, there was very little psychological research on worrying, and worrying was often considered to be synonymous with anxiety.

WORRY FACT 2. Through a process of "ex-consequentia" reasoning (the assumption of danger in the presence of anxiety), feelings of anxiety may be used to validate irrational thoughts and generate hypothetical worries.

Anxiety is an emotion—one that we experience like many other emotions in life. Let's be clear: Emotions are not part of us simply to be "felt" or "experienced." They're not with us simply to provide a "different" way of experiencing the world. Emotions have evolved as a central feature of human nature because they serve a function—an evolutionary function. Individual emotions facilitate reproductive success or help us identify and deal with specific challenges to reproductive fitness, and that's why, after thousands of years of human evolution, we still experience emotions. And anxiety is no exception.

But before we can begin to understand anxiety, we have to understand what fear is. This is because fear responses form at least some of the experience that we call anxiety. Fear is a very basic emotion, and many of our fear reactions to *immediate* threats are reflexive responses that have been biologically prewired over many thousands of years of selective evolution.

You're bound to be familiar with the basic fear reactions—the sudden startle reactions and physiological arousal that are triggered by things like loud noises, looming shadows, sudden sharp pain, rapid movements toward you, and even staring eyes![88] We all get startled by loud noises at firework displays (and so do our dogs and cats). Our attention is immediately grabbed when we see an animal darting backward and forward in our peripheral vision. And how weird is that rush of adrenaline when we dare to look up when riding the subway and see someone staring at us? You don't learn these reactions. You're born with them, but did you spot the common link between all those diverse triggers for our reflexive fear responses?

The triggers are all characteristics possessed by most predatory animals when they're about to pounce—the looming shadow, the rapid movement toward you, and the staring eyes as the predator fixates its prey. With survival from predators being a very urgent business indeed, prewired reflexive responses that make you alert to and avoid these physical threats have evolved. And evolution is a very efficient process, so it wouldn't necessarily give you built-in reflexes that respond to every individual predator you might possibly encounter. Rather, it selects out characteristics that are common to most predators and provides you with immediate reactions to these universal features.

All of that is fear, but anxiety is a little different. The modern world is made up of many more potential threats and challenges than predatory animals, so we've developed a more flexible system for managing potential threats, and this is what anxiety is. Anxiety is not a response to immediate threats (like avoiding a charging bull in a field), but a response to future anticipated threats and challenges (like a presentation you're due to give for a job interview next week). It's a bit like fear, but with many extra bells and whistles.

While you can think of fear as reflexes that evolved to deal with immediate threats, anxiety is best conceived as an emotion related to the motivational systems devoted to fear but that develops into a broader "precautionary system" with additional higher-level cognitive activities. For instance, you likely recognize the basic fear ingredients involved in anxiety: increased heart rate, cortical arousal (sharper attention to things that may be threatening), high autonomic nervous system reactivity (being more aroused and ready to react), and partial freezing and inhibition of ongoing responses (your mind going blank when you're anxiously giving an important presentation).

To these fundamental defining features are then added a range of basic psychological processes that influence attentional focus, and cautious, defensive interpretations of ongoing events.[89] These higher-level cognitive processes involved in anxiety have a number of effects that result in us being much more cautious in what we think and what we do, and as I'll describe in more detail later, this is where anxiety begins to influence our worrying.

Anxiety gives our higher-level cognitive processes a hefty nudge toward greater caution. But how does it do this? Well, it affects a number of our most influential cognitive processes, such as attention and decision making, and it does this in ways that you're probably not consciously aware of.

Let's begin with decision making. Consider the sentence "Corinne opened her weekly pay stub and was surprised at what she found." Now, I want you to make a quick, snap decision about that sentence: Was it a good thing or a bad thing? Some of you may have said it was a good thing, and some of you may have said it's a bad thing. That's because the sentence is inherently ambiguous when it comes to judging its valence. For example, Corinne may have been surprised because she found more money in her pay than she expected (a good thing) or because there was less money (a bad thing). But if you're experiencing anxiety, you're more likely to make a negative or threatening interpretation of an ambiguous sentence like this.[90]

Much of what happens in our daily lives is ambiguous, especially when we encounter the behaviors, conversations, and expressions of others, and anxiety tips us toward jumping to more negative conclusions about these and many other of our daily experiences. But not only does anxiety make us interpret ambiguity more negatively and cautiously, it also has a more immediate impact on our attentional processes.

In the 1980s, one of the first things that anxiety researchers discovered was that anxiety had an important effect on our attentional processes. Basically, if you were anxious, you were significantly more likely to switch your attention to things around you that were potentially threatening or challenging. And this attention switch would occur before you'd become consciously aware of it.[91] Have you ever suddenly felt an adrenaline rush, and then turned your head to see that someone you didn't want to meet had walked into the room? This is the anxiety attention bias—the adrenaline rush indicates your brain noticed this person even before you were consciously aware of who it is. This is anxiety keeping you alert to threats and challenges, and if anxiety had a motto, it would most likely be, "Better to be safe than sorry."

Another interesting fact about anxiety is that anxiety tricks you into thinking something bad is likely to happen. And it does this by affecting our reasoning processes. When we experience anxiety, our brain will often reason that "if I'm feeling anxious, then there must be danger." The fancy name for this is the "ex-consequentia reasoning fallacy,"[92] and it's basically a reasoning fallacy because anxious individuals often use their feelings of anxiety to validate irrational thoughts and hypothetical worries that their catastrophizing has invented. For example, if you believe that you forgot to turn off the stove before you left home (a hypothetical worry), then, if you're anxious, you'll use your anxiety as evidence that you probably did leave the stove on (this is the ex-consequentia reasoning fallacy). You can imagine how this can become a vicious cycle as anxiety implies the presence of danger, which creates distress, which is itself then interpreted as more anxiety, implying even more danger—a breeding ground for irrational, improbable, and fallacious worries. This is just one example of how anxiety can both generate hypothetical worries and make you think they're real.

In summary, anxiety is an emotion that's evolved to protect you. When we're anxious, our attention becomes drawn toward potential threats, we are more likely to interpret ambiguous events as being threatening, and we deploy reasoning processes that maintain threatening interpretations of events. Bearing these features in mind, let's look at how worrying is different from anxiety and how a mixture of worrying and anxiety can turn you into a catastrophic worrier—a situation where your worrying progresses well beyond the call of normal duty.

Worry and Anxiety—Vive la Différence!

WORRY FACT 3. Anxiety-free worry is associated with "positive" characteristics, such as problem-focused coping strategies and an information-seeking cognitive style.

WORRY FACT 4. Anxiety per se is associated with characteristics that often lead to poor psychological outcomes, such as poor problem-solving confidence, poor perceived control over problems, taking responsibility for negative but not for positive outcomes, a tendency to define events as threats, and avoidance and emotion-focused coping strategies.

Together with colleagues James Hampton, Jola Farrell, and Sue Davidson at the City University in London, one of the first worry studies I conducted was designed to establish the possible differences between anxiety and worry.[93] We already knew that anxiety was an emotion, whereas worry was a cognitive activity. But we wanted to know if there were any defining features that clearly made worrying distinct from anxiety. Given what little evidence was available at the time, we decided to throw the kitchen sink at this.

We conducted a survey asking participants questions about a broad range of things—not just their worrying and levels of anxiety, but also the types of coping strategies they used, their experience of mental health problems, and their use of cognitive strategies we knew to be risk factors for anxiety-based mental health problems. Once our filing cabinets were heaving with data, we used statistical techniques to discover what worry looked like when we stripped it of anything associated with anxiety. And we did the same to anxiety: What did anxiety look like when we stripped it of anything related to worry?

When you look at worry and anxiety in this way, they turn out to be quite different things. Anxiety-free worry was characterized by the use of adaptive, problem-focused coping strategies and an information-seeking cognitive style and—perhaps surprisingly—also with avoidance coping and emotion-focused coping (attempts to regulate stress during exposure to negative events).

However, when anxiety was stripped of any factors related to worry, it was a completely different kettle of fish. Worry-free anxiety was characterized by several psychological processes that are normally considered to result in poor psychological outcomes. These included poor problem-solving confidence, poor perceived personal control over problems, beating yourself up by taking responsibility for negative but not for positive outcomes, a tendency to define events as threats, and avoidance and emotion-focused coping strategies. This is anxiety trying to keep you safe but making you paranoid and distressed in the process—a strategy that probably works, but at a psychological cost.

It's hard to avoid seeing these results in a black-and-white way. Worrying was associated largely with very positive traits, such as use of adaptive problem-focused coping (dealing with a problem by trying to find a solution to it) and an information-seeking cognitive style (seeking information to inform you about a problem). In contrast, measures of anxiety were associated largely with processes considered to result in poor psychological outcomes, which ultimately could give rise to anxiety-based mental health problems. What jumps out when you consider these findings is that worry appears to be "good" and anxiety is "bad"! So where does it all go wrong? Why are some forms of worry, such as catastrophic worrying, such a distressing and unproductive process for some people and not the positive, productive activity that our study seemed to imply?

The Anxious Worrier

WORRY FACT 5. Worrying while feeling anxious introduces factors into the worry process that can act to thwart effective problem solving.

WORRY FACT 6. Worrying while anxious leads the anxious worrier to actively seek threats even in events that may seem to be unambiguously positive.

WORRY FACT 7. The lack of confidence in problem solving caused by anxiety leads the anxious worrier to vacillate and prolongs their worrying.

WORRY FACT 8. The inability of anxious worriers to evaluate potential solutions to worries often leads them to worry equally about controllable and uncontrollable worries.

If you ask ordinary people what they think worry is, many of them would say it's simply a process where they "think through" their problems. There's no hint of agonizing, no mention of sleepless nights, and no allusions to stress or anxiety. These are probably anxiety-free worriers, applying problem-solving and information-seeking strategies to their everyday problems and finding their worry both helpful and adaptive.

But what happens to this helpful, adaptive worry process when we throw anxiety into the mix? Well, it's a bit like shoving an alligator into a room with a rabbit—it can only end messy. If pure worrying is an attempt to problem solve by thinking through possible scenarios and how you would deal with them, then when you bring anxiety to this process, you're bringing a lot of baggage that can easily thwart this adaptive process.[94] As I mentioned above, anxiety is associated with poor problem-solving confidence, poor perceived personal control, taking responsibility only for negative but not for positive outcomes, an increased tendency to define events as threats, and the deployment of avoidance or emotion-focused coping strategies—an impressive list of barriers to effective problem solving!

Let's quickly think through how some of the features associated with anxiety might thwart effective problem solving. One common characteristic of catastrophic worriers is that their worrying fails to create acceptable solutions and simply ends up defining more problems. In this case, anxiety brings both an attentional bias toward threats and an interpretation bias that leads the worrier to interpret anything that might be ambiguous as a threat—a perfect mix creating more grist for the worry mill. For our catastrophic worriers, these threat-related biases are so influential that worrying may have completely lost its problem-solving characteristics, and worry time is almost entirely spent seeking out new potential threats.

I recall a study we did looking at how chronic worriers reacted to ambiguous statements. We presented worriers with statements that represented hypothetical extracts from a diary and asked them if they thought each event was a cause for concern or not. There were three types of statements—ones that were unambiguously positive ("It's a lovely day. I find it easy to be cheerful when the sun is shining"), unambiguously negative ("I went to the hairdresser this morning, my new hairstyle is atrocious, and I look awful"), or ambiguous ("My performance in the play was commented on by everyone"). As we expected, the chronic worriers labeled a majority of the ambiguous statements as a cause for concern—reflecting their bias toward interpreting ambiguous events as threatening.

But something completely unexpected also cropped up. Chronic worriers also labeled many of what we had considered to be "unambiguously positive" statements as a cause for concern. Not only had they interpreted ambiguity in a threatening way, but they were also actively seeking downsides even in our unambiguously positive statements! For example, when questioned about why a statement like "'I've just received an invitation to my best friend Lucy's birthday party" might be a cause for concern, one of the chronic worriers replied, "because there might be strangers there that I don't know." Another claimed, "I wouldn't know what to wear." This is anxiety digging deep into the detail of an event and coming up with every scrap of evidence that something lurking there is threatening or challenging. This is one way that anxiety bullies the worry process into creating even more worries. I'll discuss this process again in chapter 9 where you'll have the opportunity to assess whether you have a negative (or maybe positive) interpretation bias.

One other way in which anxiety can thwart worry's attempts to actively problem solve is by affecting your confidence levels. I described in chapter 1 how we had experimentally identified poor problem-solving confidence as a causal factor in generating catastrophic worrying, but now we can see that poor problem-solving confidence is in fact a characteristic linked to anxiety rather than worrying per se. So, if we put worry and anxiety together, we often get a form of vacillation that merely prolongs the period spent worrying. If the drive to worry is confronted by a lack of problem-solving confidence that is a result of anxiety, we end up with copious attempts at problem solving and information seeking but an unwillingness to accept the generated solutions as acceptable ones.

This clash of worry with anxiety helps explain why the catastrophic worrier often vacillates from solution to solution while worrying and the fact that anxious worriers also appear to have unrealistically high-evidence expectations and take longer to evaluate ambiguous sentences.[95] That is, they require more evidence on which to base a decision—presumably as a result of their lack of confidence in their own solutions. For example, imagine the scenario where you can't find your passport and it may have been lost. There are different ways to deal with this problem, such as conducting a systematic search of your home (if you think the passport might be found) or simply applying for a new passport (if you think the passport is unlikely to be found). But the anxious worrier finds it difficult to weigh the evidence either way. This delays problem resolution and prolongs fruitless worrying. This is just another way that problematic anxiety can thwart successful problem solving.

This inability of the anxious worrier to weigh evidence and evaluate potential solutions creates a further problem. Because the anxious worrier can't make up their mind about suitable solutions, it also means they'll be relatively bad at evaluating whether a worry problem is controllable or uncontrollable. So they'll end up worrying about controllable *and* uncontrollable problems in the same way and losing a lot of sleep trying to solve problems that are effectively out of their control.

Managing Your Anxiety

If anxiety has such a toxic and disruptive effect on our worrying, then it's not rocket science to conclude that anything that can alleviate anxiety would prevent these toxic influences and help to make our worrying more positive, successful, and less distressing. In this chapter, I focused on the role that anxiety plays in generating catastrophic and perseverative worrying, so I'll end the chapter with some advice on how to manage your anxiety and anxiety-related processes that thwart successful worrying.

Anxiety can affect you in two rather different ways. First, it can be an acute condition that afflicts you for a day or so, usually depending on what has been recently happening in your life. You may have had a difficult day at work, missed your train, lost your keys, or been stuck in traffic and missed an appointment. Such experiences give rise to an acute anxiety state that we would usually describe as "stress" and is primarily characterized by the immediate physiological element that we associate with anxiety (such as arousal, high blood pressure, muscle tension, rapid breathing, hot flushes, and so forth). This is usually known as "state" anxiety because it's anxiety triggered by specific life events and may dissipate after a very short period of time.

Second, a slightly different form of anxiety is known as "trait" anxiety, and this is a more chronic type of anxiety that some people experience daily, often for lengthy periods of their life. When trait anxiety develops, it tends to be anxiety that is maintained by the way the sufferer has come to think about themselves and the world. The mind of the trait-anxious person can keep them feeling anxious even without any objective threats and challenges currently occurring in their life.[96] In many cases, this may even lead to developing very specific anxiety-based disorders, such as obsessive-compulsive disorder, panic disorder, or generalized anxiety disorder.

What follows are a set of suggestions to help you manage acute bouts of anxiety, such as those caused by daily stresses and hassles, and tips for you to consider if your anxiety is a longer-term affliction that may require changes to the way you think and behave and to your lifestyle in general.

EXERCISE 6: Boosting Your Mood

If your day has left you feeling anxious, stressed, tired, or even angry, here are some simple and handy evidence-based tips to help you lift your mood. Lifting negative moods, such as anxiety, should help prevent rumination and perseverative worrying from ruining the rest of your day.

Materials

Depending on which mood-lifting strategy you choose to use, you'll need:

  Smartphone or iPod

  Fragrant candles of your choice

  Videos that make you laugh

  Relaxing bath salts

What It Is

Evidence-based research has shown that each of the following activities can help boost your mood if you're feeling low, stressed, or just in a negative mood generally. Most negative moods are often caused by the daily events you've experienced and so can be relieved relatively quickly by engaging in a suitable mood-lifting activity.

How Will This Help My Worrying?

In chapter 1, we identified negative mood as a significant contributor to cata-strophic worrying, and it's a factor that we know will prolong any bout of worrying. In this chapter, I've also shown that anxiety is an emotion that can thwart worry-ing as a problem-solving process, so lifting negative moods in general, and anxiety in particular, will help lessen the distressing aspects of worrying and prevent wor-rying from becoming perseverative.

How to Do It

Try any of the following mood-lifting activities that you think might suit you.

- **Listen to upbeat music.** Yuna Ferguson, a psychologist from the University of Missouri, has conducted studies showing that listen-ing to upbeat or positive music can immediately boost your mood.[97] You need to have a positive association with the music, and you need to listen to the music with the intention of improving your mood, but without constantly saying to yourself, "Am I happy yet?" If you do that, it doesn't work! We've conducted lab studies where we've used positive music to make participants feel happier and less anxious. This works well for improving mood in the short term, and people tend to worry less after listening to upbeat or positive music. What's a good upbeat mood-boosting tune? Well, Dr. Jacob Jolij, a cognitive neuroscientist at the University of Groningen, has devel-oped a scientific formula for identifying the top ten feel good songs.[98] Here they are from number one down to number ten.

  1. "Don't Stop Me Now," Queen
  2. "Dancing Queen," ABBA
  3. "Good Vibrations," The Beach Boys
  4. "Uptown Girl," Billy Joel
  5. "Eye of the Tiger," Survivor
  6. "I'm a Believer," The Monkees
  7. "Girls Just Wanna Have Fun," Cyndi Lauper

8. "Living on a Prayer," Bon Jovi

9. "I Will Survive," Gloria Gaynor

10. "Walking on Sunshine," Katrina and the Waves

So, plug in the earbuds, scroll to your favorites, and enjoy upbeat happiness!

- **Take a walk around the block.** If the weather's okay and you have the time, take a short walk outside. Not only does this physically disconnect you from your current environment that may be triggering your stress and anxiety, it also provides exercise, and even the mildest exercise can improve your mood. If it's during the day, you'll also get the benefit of some daylight exposure, which we know can improve sleep problems and reduce anxiety and depression. A study by Gregory Panza, an exercise physiologist at the University of Connecticut, tracked the physical activity of 419 generally healthy middle-aged adults. Even light physical activity, such as a ten-minute walk around the block with no noticeable increase in breathing, heart rate, or sweating, was associated with an increased sense of well-being and lowered levels of depression.[99]

- **Surround yourself with calming aromas.** Light a fragrant candle or use a diffuser to create relaxing aromas around the house. There are many different aromas that are known to have a calming and anxiety-relieving effect, such as jasmine, basil, chamomile, frankincense, patchouli, and fennel, to name just a few,[100] but perhaps one of the most well-known is lavender. Davide Donelli and colleagues at the University of Parma in Italy carried out a review of ninety scientific studies investigating the effects of lavender (in any form) on anxiety and anxiety-related conditions. They found that oral administration, massage, and inhalation of lavender had positive effects on anxiety and might even be considered as a therapeutic option in some clinical settings.[101]

- **Make yourself laugh.** Laugh your worries away. When stress builds up, laughing can instantly elevate your mood, reduce pain and stress and, as an added bonus, boost immunity by decreasing stress hormones and increasing immune cells and infection-fighting antibodies. Laughing does this by releasing the natural opiate dopamine in the nucleus accumbens area of the brain—this is the reward center in the brain—and has the effect of instantly making you feel less stressed and more positive. So, on your laptop, bookmark some YouTube videos that make you laugh so you can immediately access them when you need to. Alternatively, keep some classic comedy programs on your hard drive. Laughter really is one of the best medicines (but tickling yourself doesn't work—get someone else to do that!).

- **Take a bath or shower.** Zoning out is a good thing if you can immediately create your own bit of space where you can relax peacefully. So what better than the privacy of the bath or a shower? In many cultures, bathing has been a means of relaxing and purifying the body, but lying in a hot bath can have a number of other important benefits. It improves our circulation and helps us fall asleep before bedtime, and if you're lucky enough to have a hot tub, spending ten minutes in there lowers blood pressure in people with hypertension.[102] If you're bathing at the end of the work day, then it's a relaxing and suitable place to think through your positive achievements and wash away the stresses of the day.

TIPS

There are many more suggestions for ways in which you can boost your mood—most can be found on health and well-being websites. I've highlighted just a few activities for which there is some reliable scientific evidence for their effectiveness. But since everyone is different, there may be many other activities that suit you. Some include looking through old photographs, clearing clutter in your immediate environment, cooking, chatting with a close friend, writing about your worries or negative feelings, or simply just smiling.[103]

EXERCISE 7: Ten Tips for Managing Your Anxiety

Some of us are lucky enough that stress and anxiety visit us only fleetingly. But for others, anxiety can become a chronic and distressing condition. Chronic anxiety can often emerge out of a toxic brew of negative moods, dysfunctional beliefs about yourself and the world, biased thinking, and avoidant behavior, and each of these will need attention if chronic anxiety is to be properly managed. If your anxiety is a chronic condition, you may need some longer-term strategies that will help you to manage your anxiety and get more out of your life.

Materials

Sticky notes

What It Is

Below is a list of ten tips that will help you keep an informed perspective on what anxiety is and arm you with some very basic dos and don'ts when it comes to managing your anxiety.[104] Each tip comes with a brief "message to self." Try choosing one or more of these messages and posting them at prominent points in your home, such as on the fridge or on your laptop screensaver. You want these messages to become fully integrated into your daily life.

How Will This Help My Worrying?

This chapter has been all about how anxiety and worrying are a toxic mix—anxiety thwarts successful problem solving and has other negative effects on your worrying, including making you less confident about your ability to deal with problems and making you ruminate and worry in ways that make worry seem uncontrollable. Managing your anxiety in the longer term will make your worrying seem less distressing and more under your own control.

How to Do It

Try any of the following strategies.

- **Accept that anxiety is a normal emotion and can be helpful.** Anxiety often generates additional layers of anxiety—especially if you become anxious about being anxious. As I mentioned earlier, anxiety isn't unnatural; it's a normal emotion that has evolved to be helpful. Bouts of anxiety usually don't last very long, so try not to fight your feelings of anxiety, but instead accept these feelings and say to yourself that it's okay to be anxious. *Message to self: "It's okay to be anxious."*

- **Understand that anxiety can't harm you.** Experiencing anxiety doesn't mean you're going crazy; it means you're normal. You may wrongly interpret the signs of anxiety as being possibly harmful. Anxiety is not necessarily a pleasant feeling, but anxiety is not harmful, nor is it a sign of impending illness. *Message to self: "Anxiety can't harm me; I can still do what I need to do."*

- **Check that your anxiety is justified.** Do a reality check on your anxieties. Ask yourself if what you're anxious about really is a significant threat or challenge and whether other people are anxious about the things you are. Often the thing causing your anxiety may not be as dangerous or threatening as you think. *Message to self: "Is my anxiety justified?"*

- **No one is perfect. Take a break from the rigid rules that make you anxious.** Setting the highest standards for everything, all the time, is a recipe for stress and anxiety. So try to analyze the kinds of rigid rules that you apply to yourself and replace these with more realistic expectations. These rigid, maladaptive rules are things like "I must always be loved by everyone," or "I must never let anyone down." Write down some of the rigid rules you live your life by and try to think of some more reasonable alternatives. For example, "I need to be fully in control of everything I do" could become, "I will do my best but accept that some things are out of my control." *Message to self: "No one is perfect—I will live my life using realistic rules."*

- **Avoid avoidance.** Avoidance is arguably the main factor that allows anxiety to develop and propagate. Avoiding things that make you anxious is telling your brain that you're still frightened of that thing you're avoiding. If you're avoiding things that most other people think are safe, then you may need to deal with what could be inappropriate anxiety. But you will never discover there's no monster in the closet if you continue to avoid opening the closet door. It's best to approach your anxieties in a structured, step-by-step way rather than just jumping in at the deep end. You can find a structured way to approach facing your fears in chapter 12 of my book *The Anxiety Epidemic*. *Message to self: "Anxiety feeds off avoidance. I'll try to find a way to face my fears."*

- **Refuse to let anxiety hold you back.** Anxiety will regularly prevent you from doing things that you want to do. To overcome anxiety, you'll have to undertake some challenges that initially make you feel anxious, but this can be an uplifting and valuable experience if you eventually manage to prove your anxiety wrong. Trying new things, taking on challenges, and solving problems all add up to a healthier and more productive life. *Message to self: "I will not let my anxiety hold me back."*

- **Consider being adventurous rather than avoiding risk and uncertainty.** Life is basically an adventure, and there is nothing that stymies an adventure more than trying to avoid risk and uncertainty, so try to tip the balance from avoiding risk to seeking out new experiences. Try doing something you consider adventurous at least once a week—things like going into a new situation where you don't know what will happen or doing things without seeking reassurances from others first. *Message to self: "I will do something adventurous every week."*

- **Be aware of the bigger picture.** You're not just simply your anxiety; believe it or not, there is a lot more to you. But aspects of your broader lifestyle may be colluding with your anxiety, maintaining it, and even preventing you from moving on. For example, anxiety and sleeping problems are close allies, as are depression and anxiety. Try to organize your life so you're able to get a regular good night's sleep (see exercise 5 in chapter 4 for some advice on managing sleeping problems). If you also feel depressed, get help to relieve your depression because tackling your depression may leave you more confident to overcome your anxiety. Becoming overreliant on anxiety medication or even choosing to drown your anxiety in alcohol is also unlikely to help you move on from anxiety. Excessive drinking can leave you with hangovers that mean you miss work or school, it increases secretion of the anxiety-generating hormone cortisol, and it physically creates low mood and feelings of nausea and confusion—all sensations that trigger anxious thinking and anxious cognitive processes. Finally, you should encourage yourself to embrace healthy living. Regular exercise is known to reduce anxiety, and a healthy diet is associated with better mental health. *Message to self: "I'll try to embrace a healthier lifestyle and move on from anxiety."*

- **Recruit help.** Moving on from anxiety will require you to change a lot of things you do and the way you do them, so it's always helpful to enlist the help of family or friends to try to achieve these changes. Friends may help you to attempt things you've never done before because of your anxiety, and it's also good to know that other people understand your anxiety problems and are willing to help you. *Message to self: "I'm happy to ask friends and family to help me to achieve changes that will reduce my anxiety."*

- **Seek professional help if you feel you need it.** Tackling your anxiety problems on your own can be a daunting and overwhelming prospect, and you shouldn't be afraid to seek more structured support from a CBT therapist, psychotherapist, or a counselor. If your anxiety is particularly distressing, seek professional help. You may be able to find suitable psychotherapeutic help privately, or alternatively, you can ask your physician or family practitioner for advice. *Message to self: "I will seek professional help if my anxiety becomes distressing or disabling."*

TIPS

Some people with chronic anxiety get relief with anxiolytic medications. These can reduce your levels of arousal and help manage your body's reaction to anxiety triggers and stressors. But pharmaceuticals won't change the way you think, nor will they significantly change your behavior in relation to your anxiety. However, if you're unsure whether you should take medications for your anxiety, you should consult your physician or family practitioner. They may even be able to refer you to the services for longer-term counseling or psychotherapy if your anxiety is particularly distressing and prevents you from working or studying.

The Collision That Creates Catastrophizing

In this chapter, we looked at how worry and anxiety are relatively independent and different processes. In its purest form, worrying is the deployment of problem solving and information seeking that we use in our attempts to resolve problems that occur in daily life. In contrast, anxiety is an emotion that we experience when we encounter threats and challenges in our lives. Anxiety is an evolved emotion that keeps us alert to threats and challenges by creating cognitive biases that keep us attuned to these threats. But worry and anxiety simply don't get along. Anxiety turns worry as a problem-solving activity into a process that simply defines more threats (the basis for catastrophizing). It destroys your confidence in any solutions your worrying might generate and prolongs your worrying as you vacillate between solutions because your anxiety prevents you from objectively evaluating them.

CHAPTER 7

Why Doesn't Worry Have an "Off" Switch?

The Worry Machine

Roadmap of the chapter. One of the perplexing things about chronic worry is that once you start worrying, it seems impossible to stop—you just can't get the worry out of your mind. In this chapter, we'll take a close look at why worry doesn't seem to have an "off" switch. Part of the reason for this is that many of us use implicit rules when we worry that prevent us turning off our worry. We can also become intolerant of uncertainty, which means we will only want to stop worrying when we are absolutely certain we've fully dealt with our worry—a very difficult state to achieve. The chapter ends with a couple of exercises. One will provide advice on how to develop stop rules that will better enable you to disengage from a worry bout. The other provides some ways in which you can become more tolerant of uncertainty when you worry.

It's a complex piece of machinery that churns out our worrisome thoughts. It makes us think about our worries in considerably more detail than we would about any other set of thoughts, and worries can readily and simply push other thoughts out of the way and take over our conscious experience. We can quite easily stop thinking about how pleasant the weather is today, but we find it almost impossible to deliberately stop thinking about the bank balance that's in the red.

So what are the elements that make up the cogs in this worry machine? The first element is our anxiety or stress. As I described in chapter 6, anxiety causes our brain to automatically bias attention toward threatening or challenging things. It also biases us toward interpreting ambiguous information as threatening. This is the start of the process where our brain begins to activate potential worries before we've even become consciously aware of them. The worry machine's "on" switch regularly gets flipped without us noticing, but what happens when we try to switch it off? To our dismay, there doesn't even appear to be an "off" switch anywhere on that wacky machine! Your worry is a runaway train heading down a steep mountain with no brakes.

How did the "off" switch get lost? Surely there was one there originally. Well, there are a number of factors that contribute to your inability to deliberately switch off your worrying. Some of these factors relate to the fact that you likely often conduct your worrying while you're in a negative mood—but I'll come back to this shortly. First, let's look at some of the rules by which you manage your worrying. Yes, you didn't realize it, but you've probably developed a set of rules that implicitly prevent you from turning off your worrying.

Worry Stop Rules

WORRY FACT 1. When worrying, chronic worriers deploy implicit goal-directed stop rules that drive them to continue worrying until they've fully explored all aspects of their worry.

WORRY FACT 2. Chronic worriers usually bring a negative mood with them to their worrying, often an anxious one. This negative mood acts as an indication that they haven't yet achieved their goal of fully exploring their worry and so must continue with their worrying.

Imagine you just woke up on a Saturday morning and you decided to clean the kitchen. You'd probably start this task with an implicit rule about when you might decide to stop. For example, you might be thinking, *I'm going to clean the kitchen until I'm sure it's perfectly clean and tidy,* or alternatively, you might be thinking, *I'm going to clean the kitchen until I don't feel like doing it any more.* These are known as "stop rules," and when you begin most activities, you have in your mind a stop rule you use to decide when to stop that activity. You won't actually verbalize these rules; they'll be implicit rules that you've learned to use when you're involved in a wide range of tasks. The first of the two examples above is known as a "goal-directed rule" because it determines what the goal of the activity is—in this case making sure the kitchen is properly clean. The second rule is called a "feel like stopping" rule because it's not concerned with how clean the kitchen is. Rather, it's a stop rule based entirely on how you feel regardless of how clean the kitchen is.

Now, let's imagine that you had a few glasses of wine too many on Friday evening. You're cleaning the kitchen on Saturday morning, and you feel rotten—throbbing head, nauseous, and tired. How do you think those two different types of stop rules will be interpreted in this scenario? In the case of the "feel like stopping" rule, you'll probably stop cleaning the kitchen quite quickly because the answer to the implicit question, Do I feel like cleaning the kitchen anymore? is almost certain to be no. However, in the case of the goal-directed stop rule, you may continue cleaning the kitchen longer because in response to the implicit question, Is the kitchen perfectly clean and tidy yet? your mood and physical condition would be irrelevant.

But this particular scenario has an added twist to it. How do you judge whether the kitchen is perfectly clean and tidy? Many people will default this decision to their mood: if my mood is bad or negative, it's not yet perfectly clean and tidy; if my mood is good or positive, then it's probably done to my satisfaction. So if you're using a goal-directed stop rule, your hangover may make you persist at cleaning the kitchen because the hangover is saying, "You don't feel good yet, so the kitchen's not perfectly clean yet." What's the moral to this story? If you want a very clean kitchen, clean it using a goal-directed stop rule while in a negative mood!

Just like cleaning the kitchen, worrying is also an activity in which you need some rules to help you decide when to stop. In a study conducted at the University of Sussex, we asked 104 participants to complete a checklist of worry stop rules that were either goal-directed rules or feel-like-stopping rules. We also asked them to complete a questionnaire that measured how much they worried. We found a very strong correlation between the use of goal-directed stop rules and frequency of worrying.[105]

Basically, people who worried more tended to report using goal-directed worry stop rules. Not only did they worry more, but they also persevered longer at a worry task than individuals who didn't use goal-directed stop rules. Worriers reported using stop rules such as "I feel I must focus on every conceivable solution to the worry before I stop" and "I must sort out everything to do with this worry before I stop." It looked as if the pathological worriers were absolute perfectionists when it came to worrying, unable to quit the process until everything seemed right.

The Magic Trick That Turns Worriers into Nonworriers

WORRY FACT 3. When chronic worriers switch from a goal-directed worry rule to a feel-like-stopping rule, it significantly reduces their tendency to catastrophize and persevere with a worry bout.

So, deploying a goal-directed stop rule for your worrying seems like it'll automatically lead you to worry for longer—the stricter your goal-directed worry rules are, the more you'll have trouble ending your worry bout. But what happens if you add a negative mood to this mix, like we did with our kitchen cleaning example earlier? Well, you can get some quite bizarre effects.

In a study I conducted with colleague Helen Startup at the University of Sussex, we recruited a group of high worriers and a group of low worriers.[106] Not unexpectedly, we found that the high worriers were all significantly more anxious than the low worriers. We then asked both groups to complete our catastrophizing interview while deliberately using a goal-directed stop rule ("I must continue to worry until I feel I've fully explored my worry"). Again, as we expected, we found that the high worriers persevered at the worry interview task for significantly longer than the low-worry group.

Why is this? One answer is that the high worriers bring a negative mood with them to the worry task—in this case their anxiety. Just like our kitchen example earlier, the high worriers' anxiety acts as information that they haven't yet achieved their goal of fully exploring their worry, so they simply keep persevering with their worrying. On the other hand, the low worriers have very low anxiety, so they're able to believe they've achieved their worry goals much sooner than the high worry group.

Now comes the interesting twist. What happens when you ask both high and low worriers to worry while deliberately using a feel-like-stopping rule? Strangely enough, we immediately turned high worriers into low worriers, and low worriers into high worriers: low worriers persevered longer at the worry interview than high worriers! You can see this illustrated in the image below. On the left, we can see that the high-worry group perseveres for more catastrophizing steps than the low-worry group when using goal-directed worry rules. But on the right, there is a dramatic switch, and the low-worry group is now persevering at the worry interview for longer than the high-worry group. We've suddenly cured high worriers of their inherent tendency to persevere at a worry task and turned the normally placid low worriers into compulsive worrywarts!

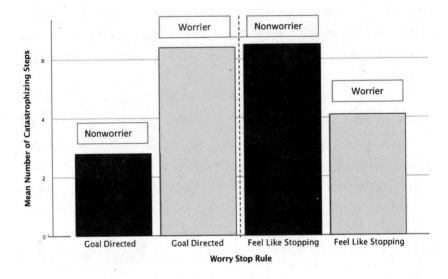

The mean number of catastrophizing steps completed by participants who were asked to use a goal-directed stop rule (left columns) or a feel-like-stopping stop rule (right columns). The light bars represent "high" worriers, and the shaded bars represent "low" worriers.

The reason for this dramatic switch in worry perseveration is because, when implicitly asking themselves if they feel like stopping, the anxiety experienced by the high-worry group is telling them, "Your mood is negative, so you don't feel like continuing," so they stop much sooner than the low-worry group who are experiencing much lower levels of negative mood.

Have we suddenly invented a spectacular cure for catastrophic worrying? Sadly, we haven't. We've certainly discovered some of the conditions under which we can change a chronic worrier's tendency to persevere at their worrying, but this was a manipulation undertaken in the strictly controlled conditions of our research lab. Once our high worriers walked out of the lab, they would almost certainly be back to their old ways, deploying their strict, goal-directed rules that would make their worry seem incessant and uncontrollable. However, don't despair, you can use the following exercise to assess your own use of goal-directed worry stop rules versus feel-like-stopping rules. This exercise also provides some tips on how to switch to less goal-directed stop rules to lessen your tendency to persevere with a worry bout.

EXERCISE 8: Identify and Change Your Implicit Worry Rules

The implicit stop rules you deploy for your worrying can determine how long you'll persevere with your worrying. If you tend to use goal-directed rules, you'll tend to persevere with your worrying until you've met some very strict criteria for stopping—such as convincing yourself that you've covered every eventuality that might occur with that worry. Alternatively, if you mainly use feel-like-stopping rules, you'll tend to stop worrying earlier regardless of whether you feel you've fully dealt with your worry or not.

Materials

Pencil or pen

Worry Stop Rule Worksheet (described below and available for download from http://www.newharbinger.com/50348)

Sticky notes

What It Is

This exercise has two purposes: first, to measure how much you use goal-directed worry stop rules and second, to provide you with some tips for how to switch to feel-like-stopping rules if your goal-directed rules are too strict.

How Will This Help My Worrying?

Most people tend to use some form of goal-directed rules for worrying (that is, most people are concerned about whether they've managed to create some solutions for the worry). But the stricter your goal-directed rules, the more likely you are to have trouble ending your worrying—especially if you're in a negative mood. This exercise is designed to help you identify and change your own worry stop rules to ones that will make your worrying less perseverative and, as a consequence, seem more controllable.

How to Do It

Measure your worry stop rule use. When people are worrying, they often say things to themselves that will *either* make themselves persevere with their worrying *or* give up on their worrying. Think back to times when you have been worrying about something and were deciding whether to continue or stop worrying. For each statement below, use the following 1-to-5 scale to rate how frequently you use the stop rule (or how often you have that particular thought).

1 = This is not the kind of thing I think of at all.

2 = I think of this a little.

3 = I think of this moderately often.

4 = I think of this quite a bit.

5 = I think of this kind of thing a lot.

_____ I must keep trying to think about what I should do if this thing happens. (GD)

_____ I can't just sit back and forget about it; this problem is serious. (GD)

_____ I must find a solution to this problem, so keep thinking about it. (GD)

_____ Stop worrying; things always work out for the best. (FLS)

_____ This may never happen, so forget about it. (FLS)

_____ I must keep thinking about this. What if I have forgotten something important? (GD)

_____ Worrying isn't going to solve anything, so forget it. (FLS)

_____ What's done is done. So what's the point in worrying? (FLS)

_____ If I don't think this issue through properly, it's not worth me doing anything else. (GD)

_____ I don't have time to think about this now. (FLS)

_____ Don't worry about it; things will get better. (FLS)

_____ I must try to think about the worst possible outcome, just in case   (GD)
it happens.

_____ No sense in worrying; I'll be okay.   (FLS)

_____ Stop worrying. In the long run, this just won't matter very much.   (FLS)

_____ I must think everything through properly.   (GD)

_____ I should just spend a little bit more time thinking this over.   (GD)

_____ Things will be okay, and worrying will not help anything.   (FLS)

_____ I must keep worrying about this; otherwise, things won't get done   (GD)
properly.

_____ If I continue thinking about this problem, then I will be actively   (GD)
able to change what is happening to me.

When you've finished rating each statement, add up all your scores for the GD items (goal-directed items) and then do the same for FLS items (feel-like-stop-ping items). You should end up with two scores: a total score for GD items and a total score for FLS items.

If the implicit stop rules you're using are too strict and may be contributing to your tendency to worry, you can try switching to the explicit use of some feel-like-stopping rules.

Choose three feel-like-stopping (FLS) rules from the list—ones that you think might be effective in helping you stop worrying whenever you find yourself stuck in a bout of worrying and unable to stop.

It's important that you become familiar with these new FLS worry stop rules and integrate them into your daily life as well as you can. Some tips on how to do this are provided in the "Tips" section.

TIPS

How to interpret your score:

- You'll probably find that your goal-directed (GD) score is higher than your feel-like-stopping (FLS) score. That's not unusual, even for people who are not chronic worriers. However, if your GD score is above 28, then you're scoring higher than the average person on the use of goal-directed worry stop rules.

- If your goal-directed stop rule (GD) score is higher than 35, then you're probably using very strict goal-directed stop rules for your worrying—rules that may make you persevere with your worrying to the point where it becomes distressing.

- You can check whether your strategy of changing to feel-like-stopping (FLS) stop rules is working by completing the worry stop rule questionnaire again after three to four weeks of practicing your new stop rules and seeing if your goal-directed (GD) score has fallen.

How to integrate your new feel-like-stopping worry stop rules into your life:

- Place one or two of these rules in prominent places around you at home (such as on the fridge or on a screensaver on your laptop).

- Get into the habit of using these rules whenever you can in your daily life. For example, when you're worried that a bad thing is likely to happen, try to think about that worry in the context of one or more of your new stop rules.

- Each day choose one of your new worry stop rules and think about how that rule might influence how you do things and how you think about things on a daily basis.

- Take some time to think about what your core goals are in life (such as "to have a happy and contented relationship with my partner" or "to have a successful work career") and think about how your new stop rule might help you to achieve these goals.

Why Are Bad Moods Bad for Worrying?

WORRY FACT 4. Negative mood actually *facilitates* performance on tasks that require systematic processing of individual elements of a problem.

WORRY FACT 5. Worrying can be viewed as a form of systematic information processing, and the two appear to share similar functional brain characteristics and are both activities found predominantly in the left hemisphere where systematic, verbal processing of information occurs.

WORRY FACT 6. Negative mood states are associated with increased performance standards, which make you more determined to achieve your goals successfully.

I mentioned briefly in chapter 1 that negative mood actually *facilitates* performance on analytical tasks. To study the effect of negative mood on the ability to analyze a problem, Joseph Forgas and Rebekah East from the University of New South Wales divided 117 student participants into three groups. Those in the positive-mood group watched an excerpt from a British comedy series, those in the neutral-mood group watched a nature documentary, and those in the negative-mood group watched an edited excerpt from a film about dying of cancer. They were then asked to watch deceptive or truthful interviews with individuals who denied committing a theft. Those in the negative-mood group were the most accurate in detecting deceptive communications, and those in the positive group were most trusting and gullible.[107]

In general, this effect occurs because negative mood makes us process information in a more detailed, systematic way, whereas positive mood tends to make us take shortcuts in our analytical thinking by using heuristics and stereotypes. As I mentioned in chapter 1, a heuristic is a mental shortcut that allows us to solve problems and make judgments quickly—but as a consequence, we may make the wrong decision!

What's all this got to do with worry? Well, quite a lot, actually. Most chronic or pathological worrying occurs while we're in a negative mood. We may be stressed, anxious, sad, tired, in pain…or even hungover! That negative mood has a lot to answer for. It contributes to perseverative worrying in a number of different ways and helps to make our worry seem uncontrollable.

First, as we've already noted, negative mood activates a systematic form of information processing that simply isn't going to allow you to use shortcuts to come to conclusions about your worry. You're going to have to go through everything—fact by fact, scenario by scenario, catastrophic outcome by catastrophic outcome! Worrying and systematic information processing appear to share similar functional brain characteristics. Systematic processing appears to be supported by functionally distinct brain processes located in the left frontal lobes, and studies show that increases in worrying are also associated with increased left-hemisphere activation in the frontal lobes. So both are predominantly left-hemisphere activities involved in the systematic, verbal processing of information.[108]

Secondly, negative mood states are associated with increased performance standards. They make you more determined to achieve your goals successfully, and this is consistent with the fact that most worriers do their worrying under strict goal-directed rules. Walter Scott and Daniel Cervone from the University of Wyoming divided undergraduate students into either a negative- or a neutral-mood condition by asking them to listen to a recording. In the negative-mood condition, they were instructed to imagine a scenario in which their best friend was dying of cancer; in the neutral-mood scenario, they were instructed to imagine visualizing their room at home. After this, all participants were asked to complete an irrelevant task in which they had to rate the meanings of presented words. But the real purpose of the study was contained in a questionnaire consisting of four items that had participants rate the minimum standard of performance with which they would be satisfied across a range of tasks (for example, "Given your GPA for this semester, what is the minimum level of performance you'd have to get this semester to be satisfied with how you'd done?"). As expected, the negative mood group reported a higher minimal standard of performance than the neutral group.[109]

This has a number of consequences for worriers who are in a negative mood. Once your criteria for successful worrying are increased by your negative mood, the length of the worry bout will extend until you feel satisfied that those more stringent criteria have been met. Sadly, these more stringent criteria for successful worrying are often never met, leading to ever more lengthy bouts of worrying in order to try and reach the unreachable. This is negative mood instilling the worry process with a hefty dose of perfectionism by raising minimum standards for successful worrying. And we know that perfectionism is very closely linked to both chronic worrying and the symptoms of generalized anxiety disorder (GAD; which were discussed in more detail in chapter 4).[110]

All these effects of negative mood, of course, occur out of conscious awareness. Otherwise, we might be able to simply tell ourselves to stop worrying, and that would be the end of it. But chronic worriers practice their art a lot—so much that most of the cognitive processes involved in worrying occur automatically. Once a threat or challenge is identified, these trigger well-rehearsed and habitual goal-directed worrying in an automatic fashion.[111]

Intolerance of Uncertainty

WORRY FACT 7. Intolerance of uncertainty is a state that's highly associated with pathological and catastrophic worrying.

WORRY FACT 8. Chronic worriers often manage their intolerance of uncertainly by either procrastinating about decisions or handing responsibility for decisions over to someone else.

WORRY FACT 9. One group of individuals whose worry and anxiety is related to intolerance of uncertainty is those with a diagnosis of autism spectrum disorder.

I mentioned in chapter 5 that one of my grandmother's favorite sayings was "There's only one thing that's certain in life—and that's uncertainty." So, do we accept uncertainty as something we have to tolerate in life? Many of us do not. If you're a chronic or a catastrophic worrier, you're not going to let something as disruptive as uncertainty get in your way. You're going to spend much of your time fruitlessly worrying about how to obtain that unobtainable state of certainty and create a whole new set of worries along the way.

Those of us who are pathological worriers often develop a psychological aversion to uncertainty, yet there will always be an element of uncertainty in every worry that plagues us. This is a state that psychologists call "intolerance of uncertainty," and it's a trait that is highly associated with pathological and catastrophic worrying. It's a state that is also a primary feature of GAD (the anxiety disorder whose cardinal characteristic is distressing, uncontrollable worrying).[112]

Intolerance of uncertainty has been compared to an allergic reaction. Dan Grupe at the University of Wisconsin–Madison explains it like this: "If you're allergic to nuts and you have a piece of birthday cake that has a drop of almonds in it, you have a violent physical reaction to it. A small amount of a substance that's not harmful to most people provokes a violent reaction in you. Intolerance of uncertainty is like a psychological allergy."[113] When someone who is intolerant of uncertainty is exposed to just a little bit of uncertainty, they will have a disproportionately strong reaction to it. Not only will that cause worrying, but it will also result in a strong emotional reaction, creating stress and anxiety.

If a state of 100 percent certainty is impossible to achieve, then where does this leave the worrier who's intolerant of uncertainty? Well, it probably leaves them locked in a cycle of endless worrying that's psychologically impossible to terminate. Being dissatisfied with uncertainty will give rise to the worrier's classic "What if...?" questioning in a vain attempt to close that gap in the circle left by uncertainty, and in the process, this will generate many more hypothetical worries mostly about things that will never happen. This is how worrying begins to feel uncontrollable, and this is yet another factor that makes worry seem like it just cannot be switched off.

Then how do those who are intolerant of uncertainty get out of this vicious worry cycle? They don't simply stop worrying, because worry for them doesn't have an "off" switch. Instead, they employ strategies that either distract them from their worry or very cleverly diffuse responsibility for the worry. But these strategies don't resolve the worry; they simply lessen the distressing levels of anxiety caused by uncertainty. For example, some people protect themselves from uncertainty by keeping themselves as busy as possible—thus limiting the uncertainty they might be exposed to. Others may distract themselves from their worry or simply procrastinate. If you procrastinate and decide not to do something, you don't have to feel uncertain about it!

But the canniest strategy is to diffuse responsibility by getting someone else to make a decision about the uncertainty. In its most common form, this is excessive reassurance seeking—asking someone else their opinion on a decision you find difficult to make because you can't resolve the uncertainty associated with the decision. "Should I take an umbrella out with me today?" you ask your partner. "No," your partner replies. But you can't stop yourself from then saying, "Are you sure?" You're just double-checking that the response is reliable. The individual who is intolerant of uncertainty has a lot to gain from this strategy. It reduces the anxiety caused by the uncertainty, and it also removes the responsibility for the decision. But you can bet your life that if it ends up raining, the worrier will end up blaming their partner for making the wrong decision. Your partner won't be happy.

It's clear that intolerance of uncertainty is a major factor in making worry seem uncontrollable and unstoppable, and simply trying to worry uncertainty away is an unachievable task. Because it's impossible to get rid of all uncertainty in your life, you have to learn to live with it, and exercise 9 at the end of this chapter provides some tips on learning to live with uncertainty.

This now raises the question of how some people become intolerant of uncertainty. Well, we don't know for sure. One group of individuals who are more likely to develop an intolerance of uncertainty are those with a diagnosis of autistic spectrum disorder (although not everyone with autism will have high levels of intolerance of uncertainty). There is evidence to suggest that relatively high levels of anxiety and worrying in autistic individuals may be caused in part by this increased tendency to develop intolerance of uncertainty.[114] Given that studies have shown that a diagnosis of autistic spectrum disorder is predictive of intolerance of uncertainty,[115] are there any characteristics of autism that might help us understand how intolerance of uncertainty develops? Caroline Joyce and colleagues at the University of Newcastle in the UK have speculated that the prevalence of intolerance of uncertainty in young people with autism may be a result of some of the core characteristics of autism, such as a preference for sameness and routines and difficulty adjusting to change in a neurotypical world.[116]

However, while individuals with a diagnosis of autism often exhibit high levels of intolerance of uncertainty, they are certainly not the only people who develop this aversion to uncertainty. Most recently, intolerance of uncertainty has been recognized as a risk factor not only for pathological worrying, but for many other mental health problems, such as anxiety, depression, obsessive-compulsive disorders, GAD, and eating disorders.[117] Its reach appears to be truly transdiagnostic, and intolerance of uncertainty may turn out to be lurking in the background of many common mental health problems.

EXERCISE 9: Learning to Live with Uncertainty

I've described how an intolerance of uncertainty can lead to repetitive and catastrophic worrying in a vain attempt to try to achieve certainty on a problem. This can often be quite distressing—especially if you've come to treat uncertainty as something that is aversive and a state that should be actively avoided if it can't be resolved.

Materials

Pencil or pen

Paper or notebook

Sticky notes

What It Is

In this exercise, you will look at your habits around uncertainty and worrying, evaluate and track them, and finally learn to build tolerance of uncertainty through affirming principles and reinforcement.

How Will This Help My Worrying?

If you believe that uncertainty is always a bad thing, then it will inevitably lead to you worrying. This exercise is designed to help you change negative beliefs about uncertainty to beliefs that are more in line with reality—that is, uncertainty has as many good outcomes as it does bad. But for this to happen, you need to properly integrate these new beliefs into your daily life, and the following are some practical ways you can do this.

How to Do It

Look at the following questions. These behaviors are all things that someone who is intolerant of uncertainty might do. Do you find yourself regularly doing any of these? If so, you may have developed an intolerance of uncertainty that is fueling your catastrophic worrying.

- Do you seek reassurance from others?

- Do you find yourself procrastinating regularly?

- Do you seek out lots and lots of information before making a decision about something?

- Do you find yourself double-checking things?

- Do you avoid lots of situations because you're uncertain of what might happen?

Spend the next few days keeping a record of situations in which you find yourself acting as if you're intolerant of uncertainty. Make a note of what happened and how you dealt with it. Did things turn out okay in the end even though you weren't 100 percent certain of what would happen? If there was a negative outcome, did you manage to cope with it?

To help you become more tolerant of uncertainty, study the following principles and then keep testing yourself to commit them to memory.

- Worrying only gives me the illusion of certainty because certainty is an impossible thing to achieve in life.

- Focus on the things that I can control, enjoy, or appreciate, instead of worrying about the things I can't control.

- If I'm focused on the present rather than the future, then uncertainty about the future is less likely to bother me.

- Certainty is an impossible thing to achieve in life, and worrying only gives me a false sense of certainty.

- When I predict bad things happening when I'm uncertain, it is just as likely that good things will happen.

- I will learn to tolerate any discomfort I get from uncertainty. I will notice my discomfort and then just sit with it. Being somewhat uncomfortable is not the end of the world.

- Being focused on the present (via breathing, bodily sensations, and noticing my surroundings) helps me accept uncertainty.

- Uncertainty is neutral. Something bad may happen in the future, or something great may happen.

- Instead of telling myself that I'm worried about the uncertainty of the future, I'll tell myself that I'm feeling cautious expectation and excitement.

Place one or two of the statements that you think are particularly relevant to you in prominent places around the house (such as on the fridge or on a screensaver on your laptop).

Get into the habit of using these principles whenever you can in your daily life (such as when you think a bad thing is likely to happen, try to think how a good thing might happen instead of that bad thing).

Each day, choose one principle and think about how that principle might influence how you do things and how you think about things on a daily basis (for example, "Focus on the things that I can control, enjoy, or appreciate, instead of worrying about the things I can't control").

Take some time to think about what your core goals are in life (such as "to have a happy and contented relationship with my partner" or "to have a successful work career") and think about how these principles might help you to achieve these goals.

TIP

Share these principles and discuss them with your family members, your significant other, or your best friend. The support of such people will help you practice what you preach and integrate these principles into your daily life.

Adding an "Off" Switch to the Worry Machine

In this chapter, I described some of the factors that make worry seem like it's uncontrollable and unstoppable. First, many people develop the use of worry stop rules that encourage worry perseveration. These are usually goal-directed rules that urge us to consider every aspect of our worry until we're certain we've dealt with it properly, but this is a state that is usually impossible to achieve. In addition, if we're using these very strict rules while we're in a negative mood (anxious, sad, or tired, for example), our negative mood will be telling us that we haven't yet achieved that goal of certainty yet, so we should continue worrying.

Second, in addition to using very strict goal-directed worry rules, many people also develop an aversion to uncertainty, and this intolerance of uncertainty is highly associated with pathological and catastrophic worrying. Striving to be certain is like running a marathon, but as you near the end, the finish line is constantly being moved farther away. It's exhausting and technically unachievable.

CHAPTER 8

Combat Catastrophizing by Practicing Good Worry Habits

Begin to Manage Your Chronic Worrying

Roadmap of the chapter. So far, we've discussed some of the factors that cause us to worry catastrophically. In contrast, this chapter is about establishing some positive worry habits that will help you reduce the tendency to worry pathologically. You'll start by asking questions such as: What do I worry about? Where do I worry about it? What are my worry fears? And are my worries solvable? I show you how you can reduce the negative impact of worrying on your daily life by confining your worrying to very specific periods of the day. I also offer some ways you can reduce the emotional impact of your worries. You'll meet Marlene and see how our worry exercises help her begin managing her chronic worrying.

Marlene is forty-five years old and has a partner and two children: a son in tenth grade and a daughter just out of high school. She works in an administrative role in the accounting department of a medium-sized company on the edge of town. She has a history of anxiety and depression, and she attempted suicide after the breakup of a relationship in her early twenties.

She and her family recently moved to a new, larger home, and both Marlene and her partner have been working long hours to pay the mortgage and support their children. Marlene admits that she's always been an anxious person and a bit of a worrier, and now she spends a lot of time worrying about her partner, her children, and their financial situation. On many days she says she "gets into a state" worrying about the well-being of her family and how they'll cope. She worries if they're late coming home, and sometimes this triggers worries about her relationship with her partner. She feels like her partner is about to break up with her all the time, even though she has no evidence on which to base this feeling. As a result, she resists showing any affection in case her partner might reject it.

Her catastrophic worrying now embraces even mundane everyday events, such as whether there's a stain on the carpet, whether there'll be anywhere to park when she gets to work, and what she'll do if she loses her keys while she's out—worries that feel uncontrollable. These simple, everyday worries seem to undermine her self-esteem and confidence. All this is affecting her ability to concentrate on her work, which in turn triggers worries about losing her job.

She says the continual worrying makes it feel as if there is something inside her driving her crazy, and this has led her to drinking the best part of a bottle of wine most evenings, and she reports having increasing difficulty sleeping as she inevitably takes every little stress and strain to bed with her. She says it feels like the foundations of everything are falling apart around her. She just desperately wants to stop feeling like this.

So far in this book, we've discussed some of the reasons why our worrying becomes catastrophic and how it makes us worry about things that simply never happen. This chapter introduces you to some good worry habits that will not only help you to eradicate the bad habits but also provide the basis for successful worrying and problem solving—a process that should be distress free and productive.

Good worry habits are based on a few simple activities—all designed to help you to manage your worrying and regain some influence over what often feels like an uncontrollable urge to worry. This involves (1) keeping a record of your worries, (2) understanding which of your worries are important to you and solvable, (3) working out ways to confine your worrying so it becomes a daily activity that you can compartmentalize and manage, and (4) developing some ways of thinking about your worries that will help you to minimize the negative impact your worries might be having on you.

Introducing Marlene

But first let me introduce you to Marlene, the subject of the story at the beginning of this chapter. Marlene has always been a worrier, but as you can grasp from her story, things have recently gotten worse, and her worrying now seems out of control and simply adds to her day-to-day stress. In this chapter, we're going to see how practicing good worry habits can help Marlene, and her example will provide a template for you to develop similar good worry habits and challenge your tendency to worry catastrophically.

Marlene's worrying seems to be racing out of control, and although her life is stressful and her financial concerns may be real, her worrying has extended to most things in her life, increasing her daily stress and anxiety—anxiety that may prevent her from looking objectively at ways she can manage her worries. From Marlene's story above, we can identify several things that need attention in order to alleviate Marlene's growing distress. Some of these are the following: (1) we will try to help Marlene reduce the amount of time she spends worrying each day, (2) Marlene would benefit from some strategies designed to manage her catastrophic worrying where she's making mountains out of molehills regardless of what she's worrying about, (3) it would be helpful to reduce the impact Marlene's worries have on her stress levels, and (4) Marlene would also benefit from learning how to lift her mood when, as she puts it, she "gets into a state." There are other aspects of Marlene's problems that require attention, such as her level of alcohol consumption and her inability to sleep. But some of the strategies she puts in place to help her manage her worrying will hopefully also naturally improve these other areas. But if not, we can tackle these additional problems later with some specific interventions.

Laying the Groundwork for Some Good Worry Habits

One of the first steps for managing out-of-control worrying is to begin with some exercises to understand the worrying. It's not easy to manage anything about your behavior if you don't have a good understanding of what you do and when you do it. Can you remember what you worried about yesterday? When you worried about it? What triggered it? How long you worried for? Was the worrying justified, and did it distract you from more important things? I bet you can't remember any of those things accurately, and if you can't accurately recall these kinds of details, it makes it difficult for you to know what it is you need to change and whether the changes you've made have worked. So, the first thing we'll do is begin by keeping a relatively detailed record of your worrying on a day-by-day basis.

EXERCISE 10: Keeping a Daily Worry Diary—Which Worries Actually Happen and Which Don't?

To get a balanced view of your worries, begin by keeping a worry diary in which you keep track of all the worries you have in a particular day. This will help you remember your worries and, more importantly, enable you to look back and see whether your worries were justified or not.

Materials

Pen or pencil

Notebook or Daily Worry Diary worksheet (described below and available for download from http://www.newharbinger.com/50348)

Marlene's Worry Diary (excerpted below with the full version available at http://www.newharbinger.com/50348)

What It Is

In this exercise, you'll write down all the worries you have each day—no matter how trivial or small they may seem. Try completing a Daily Worry Diary for a couple of weeks; then spend a little time reviewing the content of those diaries. Reflecting on these diaries will help you get insight into how you worry, and that insight is likely to help you begin to manage your worry and make it feel more controllable.

How Will This Help My Worrying?

Completing a worry diary will enable you to answer questions such as: Do I worry more in some situations than others? What kinds of thoughts do I have when I'm worrying? What kinds of things do I fear when I'm worrying, and are those fears justified? How do I feel when I'm worrying? Gaining insights into your worrying in this way is a first step to actively managing your worrying.

How to Do It

Download the Daily Worry Diary worksheet, or on a blank piece of paper or page in your notebook, write "Daily Worry Diary" and today's date at the top. Below that, write down a worry you had today beside the time it occurred. Write the following questions, leaving space for your answers: What am I thinking? What do I think will happen? How do I feel?

Here are a few examples from Marlene's worry diary (Marlene's full daily worry diary is included on the Daily Worry Diary worksheet):

Daily Worry Diary: July 12, 2022

8:00 am: Leaving home for work.

What am I thinking? What if the car doesn't start?

What do I think will happen? I'll be late for work and miss my meetings.

How do I feel? Anxious and stressed

9:00 am: Daughter buying a new motorcycle

What am I thinking? Motorcycles are dangerous. She'll be in an accident and killed.

What do I think will happen? I would miss her so much if she died.

How do I feel? Stressed, dread, sad

Write down all the worries you have during a single day—no matter how trivial or small they may seem—along with the time they occurred.

Try to be as specific as possible, in describing the situation, what you were thinking, what you believe the consequences of your worry topic would be, and how you were feeling.

Don't fill in the final "Did This Worry Happen?" column in the worksheet until at least a few days after you've completed that day's diary and you can look back and see if your worry was justified or not.

Try to complete a diary for five or six different days. These don't have to be five or six consecutive days, but completing five or six days will give you enough information to help you understand what you worry about and whether these worries are justified or not.

Before we try to make sense of what's in your worry diary, when you've made all the entries you want, indicate whether the worry actually happened or not. Simply answer "yes" or "no" to the question, Did this worry happen? For many worries, this should be quite simple. For example, for Marlene's *Did I leave the oven on?* worry, she will know for sure whether the kitchen burnt down or not and will be able to say yes or no! Other worries are a little more complicated. For Marlene's *Daughter buying a new motorcycle* worry, her daughter might still have an accident in the future. But, even so, if she hasn't had an accident yet, then the answer in the final column will still be no. For worries that you are genuinely unsure about, simply put a question mark (?) in the final column.

You can count up all the yeses and all the nos in the final column and compare the two figures to see what proportion of your worries are actually justified (ignore the ones you've labelled with a question mark).

Look carefully at the worries in your diaries that did not actually happen. Be honest, did your worrying actually do anything to prevent these bad things from happening? Or were they just never going to happen anyway? Ask yourself, was your worry unfounded?

This diary exercise will help you become more accurate at predicting whether your worries will happen or not, and this ability is an important factor in helping you to reduce your levels of worrying.[118]

TIPS

- If you want to show everyone what a stats whiz you are, you can work out the percentage of your worries that actually happened. For example, add up the total number of yes outcomes and divide this by the total number of worries in your diaries. Then multiply this by 100 to get the percentage of your worries that actually happen.

    (Total "yes" outcomes divided by total number of worries) x 100 = % of worries that actually happened

- If you are a chronic catastrophic worrier, the percentage of worries that actually happened will be significantly closer to 0 percent than it is to 100 percent—suggesting that you're doing a lot of unnecessary worrying.

- Research suggests that if you track the actual outcomes of your worrisome predictions and find that many of your worries do not actually happen, this will decrease your catastrophic worrying and your anxiety levels.

Try completing the Daily Worry Diary for a couple of weeks, then spend a little time reviewing the content of those diaries. Reflecting on these diaries should lead to insight into how you worry, and that insight is likely to help you begin to manage your worry and make it feel less uncontrollable. Questions you can ask include:

- **Do I worry more in some situations than others?** If you do, then perhaps you can become aware that specific situations and circumstances trigger your worrying and find ways to avoid those situations or manage your worrying when they occur. For example, you could distract yourself from worrying or delay your worrying to a daily scheduled worry time (see "Scheduling Daily Worry Time" later in this chapter).

- **What kinds of thoughts do I have when I'm worrying?** For example, are your thoughts self-depreciating, such as *I'm not good enough to do this work task properly*, or *No one will like me if I make a mess of cooking dinner?* In chapter 1, we discussed the fact that for many catastrophic worriers, worrying is a process that leads to them beating themselves up by introducing themes of personal inadequacy or low self-esteem into their worrying. Remember, these kinds of self-depreciating thoughts will only prolong your worrying, but you can begin to reduce the frequency of these kinds of thoughts by practicing "smart" worrying habits, such as those found in exercise 15 in chapter 9.

- **What kinds of things do I fear when I'm worrying, and are those fears justified?** Your Daily Worry Diary entries will give you insight into how much of your worrying is justified (how many of your worries actually happen). We know from previous research that once you become aware of how few of your worries actually happen, your catastrophic worrying lessens.

- **How do I feel when I'm worrying?** For the catastrophic worrier, a range of emotions often combine to generate feelings of distress that are overwhelming and disabling and prevent you from successfully engaging in even basic daily activities. You can also look back at your diary and see whether the feelings you experienced were justified given the eventual outcomes of those worries. This insight alone may help reduce your feelings of distress when worrying. But if you still feel you need some help managing your mood when worrying, then chapter 6 offers mood-lifting exercises you can use when you begin to worry.

Once you have insight about your worrying provided by the Daily Worry Diary, you can move on to categorizing your worries in ways that should help you to prioritize them and to begin to find practical solutions for those worries that pose genuine problems.

EXERCISE 11: Managing Your Worries by Their Ability to Be Solved

Human beings probably evolved the process we know as worrying in order to help them solve and deal with anticipated problems in their lives. But for many people, this process gets knocked off its evolutionary rails and develops into an activity that generates distress rather than solutions. One of the reasons for this derailment is that worriers often fail to distinguish between the types of worries they experience. You can distinguish your worries according to their ability to be solved, and categorizing worries in this way will help reduce catastrophic worrying and promote practical problem solving.

Materials

Pen or pencil

Worry Categories Worksheet (described below and available for download from http://www.newharbinger.com/50348)

What It Is

In this exercise, you will think about what things in your life are valued and important and also determine which of your worries are solvable and which are not.

How Will This Help My Worrying?

Worries that can't easily be solved are (1) worries about things that occurred in the past ("I lost my job"), (2) worries about things that are largely out of your control ("How badly will my children be affected in the future if global warming continues?"), and (3) hypothetical worries that haven't happened yet and may be highly unlikely to happen ("What if a drunk driver crashes into my partner's car on the way home from work?"). It's important to distinguish these potentially unsolvable worries from worries that are important to you and can be solved. This will allow you to focus your energies on things you *can* do something about. This process will help you develop your problem-solving skills and problem-solving confidence.

How to Do It

Review the Worry Categories Worksheet completed by Marlene below. She filled in this worksheet using the worry topics from her Daily Worry Diary. This worksheet contains three categories: (1) worries that are not important, (2) worries that are important and can be solved, and (3) worries that are important and cannot be solved.

Worry Categories Worksheet		
Not Important	**Important and Can Be Solved**	**Important but Cannot Be Solved**
Did I leave the oven on? (The stove might catch on fire.)	What if the car doesn't start and I'm late for work?	Daughter may be killed riding her new motorbike.
There is no food in the house (the family will shout at me).	Workmates are not talking to me during the lunch break (they may all dislike me).	Daughter hasn't responded to my texts (she may have had an accident).
I left the basement window open (which could cause a leak and the carpet will be ruined).	I can't sleep and won't be able to concentrate on work tomorrow.	Partner hasn't arrived home on time (my partner may be having an affair).

On Marlene's Worry Categories Worksheet, in the first column are the worries that Marlene has categorized as "not important." You'll see that these are specifically not things that are valued and important in her life but are primarily daily hassles that could happen to anyone any day. True, if you are a catastrophic worrier, you may catastrophize these events into "What if...?" calamitous outcomes, but these outcomes are relatively unlikely to happen.

In the second column are worries that are important and valued and represent practical problems that can either be planned for (making sure someone is available for a ride if the car doesn't start in the morning) or for which there is a practical solution (using mindfulness techniques to help you get to sleep).

In the third column are worries that are important but cannot be solved. For Marlene, these are all hypothetical worries that she has escalated into catastrophic outcomes and which can't be solved because they haven't happened and may never happen. Marlene has been brave to allocate worries about her daughter being killed on her new motorcycle and her partner returning home late to the "important but cannot be solved" category because they are worries that have particularly catastrophic consequences for her in her own mind. But this is a first step to admitting that these worries may indeed only be hypothetical, and by using the Worry Categories Worksheet, she realized that the dramatic outcomes she envisages for these worries may be extremely unlikely.

Categorize your worries from your Daily Worry Diary in the following ways:

- **Worries that are not important.** If a worry is *not* related in some way to important or valued aspects of your life, you should include that worry in this category (for example, *I broke a mug today, I forgot to buy toilet paper, I was late leaving home for work today*).

- **Worries that are important and can be solved.** These are problems that are of genuine concern to you, relate to valued aspects of your life, and have to do with practical problems currently present in your life. Ask yourself: Is this a worry I can do something about now? Is there a practical plan I can use to solve this problem? If the answer is yes to both questions, then place that worry in this category. Example worries that could be included in this category are

I'm not going to be able to finish that very important work assignment until I get my printer fixed. My debit card was stolen, so I won't be able to pay my electricity bill. My best friend was very rude to me in public recently, and I don't know how to raise this with her. All these relate to important matters in your life and can probably be solved with a little thought and effort.

- **Worries that are important and cannot be solved.** These are worries that are important to you, but you do not have the means either to control or to problem solve them. Worries in this category include (1) hypothetical worries of the "What if…?" kind that have not yet happened and may never happen (see the examples that Marlene has given in her worksheet), (2) worries about things from the past that cannot be changed, and (3) worries that you genuinely have very little ability to control. Examples include: *What if I get to work and there are no parking spaces?* (hypothetical worry) *Why did I make a fool of myself at my daughter's wedding?* (worry from the past) *What if my partner falls in love with someone else and leaves me?* (worry that you have little control over)

TIPS

- Categorizing your worries in this way will help you differentiate between the different types of worries you have. In particular, after completing this exercise, you should be actively labeling some worries as not important, and as such, you are just one step from letting those worries go. However, if you're still finding it hard to let go of those worries you've labeled as not important, you can begin the process of letting them go by allocating them to a scheduled worry time, which I'm going to describe next.

- This categorization exercise will also help you think actively about whether worries can be solved and, if so, how they might be solved. This is important because many catastrophic worriers simply agonize over their worries and only think about what further problematic outcomes a worry might be harboring (the "What if...?" catastrophizing style). There is often no attempt to think about how the problem might be solved. Identifying that a worry may be solvable is the first step to solving it, and there are exercises to help you develop problem-solving skills in chapter 9.

EXERCISE 12: Scheduling Daily Worry Time

One of the problems we identified with Marlene's worrying is that it occurs at all times of the day and night and in every kind of situation: at work, at home, and when she's in bed trying to sleep. She can move from one situation to another, but it still feels like she's taking her worries with her wherever she goes. One way to manage this perpetual worrying is to confine worrying to just one place at one particular time of day. This means worrying should be elicited less reflexively in other environments at other times of day. This will help you feel that you're beginning to regain control over your life.

Materials

Pen or pencil

Notebook

Worry Time Worksheet (described below and available for download at http://www.newharbinger.com/50348)

What It Is

This exercise is designed to help you establish a "worry time" each day. You choose a particular place and time to do your worrying each day, and you postpone all other worrying until this scheduled worry time.

How Will This Help My Worrying?

This is something that can work quite well for many catastrophic worriers. It helps you feel you're regaining some control over your worrying, and your worrying no longer feels like it's taking over your whole life.

How to Do It

First, download or draw a Worry Time Worksheet, like the one completed by Marlene below.

Worry Time Worksheet
Date: July 13, 2022
My scheduled worry time: 6:30 p.m. My worry time duration: 30 minutes
My Worries ~~What if the car doesn't start and I'm late for work?~~ My daughter could be killed riding her motorcycle. ~~I must always try to remember whether I've turned the oven off.~~ ~~My workmates don't talk to me much; maybe they all dislike me.~~ I'm always worried when my daughter doesn't respond to my texts. ~~I must always make sure there's food in the house.~~ ~~I'm always worrying that I may have left the window open and it will cause a leak.~~ When my partner is late, I worry that they might be having an affair.

Now select a suitable time and place for your worry time. Choose a time when you know you're least likely to be interrupted and when you have no other activities planned. If you work during the day, then finding some time during the evening may be suitable, but try to avoid selecting a time close to your bedtime when you might end up taking your worries into bed with you. Choose a specific duration for your worry time. Twenty or thirty minutes may be enough time. You're only going to worry for the time duration that you choose, and no longer.

Choose a place for your worry time where you're least likely to be interrupted, and let others around you know that they shouldn't disturb you. Don't forget to turn your phone off. This is your special time where you worry and do nothing else.

During the rest of the day, you will probably still find yourself worrying, but when you do, you can write your worries down in a notebook or on a Worry Time Worksheet, and postpone them until your scheduled worry time. But be aware that some worries may be too important to postpone to a later worry time and you may have to act on these immediately (for example, you will want to cancel your bank card immediately if you discover it's been lost or stolen).

Once you've written down your worry on the worksheet, try to refocus on what you were doing. I know this can be difficult, and if you can't get back into what you were doing before your worry popped into your head, then either try to distract yourself by moving on to something completely different or by engaging in a simple mindfulness exercise (like the one described in chapter 10). When you're not in your scheduled worry time, it's important that you focus on the here and now and remember that you will still have time to think about your worry during your scheduled worry time.

Begin your scheduled worry time by reading the list of worries on your Worry Time Worksheet that you recorded during the day. You may want to categorize these worries using the Worry Categories Worksheet. This will help you identify worries that are no longer important to you as well as worries that can be solved with a little bit of constructive thought and a few problem-solving skills.

Be strict and make sure you finish your worry time when the scheduled time is up. Don't get stressed about this; you have another scheduled worry time tomorrow to continue where you left off if need be. Make sure you have a distracting activity to do after your worry time (such as preparing dinner, watching an entertaining TV program, or exercising), or alternatively try some of the mood-lifting strategies in chapter 6.

It will take a little bit of time to get used to using a scheduled worry time, and you may want to adjust the worry time schedule to suit your own needs. But don't forget, the goal is to try to reduce the time you schedule for worrying over time—not increase it.

TIPS

- When you read the list of worries that you've compiled during the day, you will probably find that some of them have already been resolved, so delete them by putting a line through them. Then read the remainder of your worries and decide which ones might have a practical solution and use your worry time to try to come up with a practical solution for these worries.

- In Marlene's example Worry Time Worksheet above, you can see that during her worry time, she deleted three of her worries as being unimportant because, after some thought, she realized that these worries were unlikely to happen, and even if they did, the consequences would almost certainly not be as bad as she originally feared (the oven worry, the food worry, and the leaving the window open worry).

- After reflecting on her remaining worries, Marlene selected the worries that she thought she could find some practical solutions for. In the case of her car not starting, she decided she could seek a ride from a neighbor who worked in the same vicinity as her. She also resolved to initiate conversations with those workmates who she felt weren't talking to her very much.

- Marlene's remaining worries are all hypothetical—worries that cause her some distress, but in reality, may never happen. But if she's still worrying about these things tomorrow, she can add them to tomorrow's list and continue to consider them during tomorrow's worry time. Worry time can be useful even with hypothetical worries because it makes you consider whether the worry really is important and whether there might be some practical solution to that worry.

- The act of physically deleting your worry from a list can also be psychologically uplifting, especially if you've deliberately made a decision to do that based on your thinking during worry time.

EXERCISE 13: Downgrade Your Worries

In order to downgrade your worries, you can employ some strategies for neutralizing them or putting them into a broader, more positive perspective that, as a consequence, will minimize their stressful impacts. These strategies are known as "cognitive-neutralizing strategies" and are designed to get you thinking about suitable statements that provide a more positive perspective on the subjects of your worrying.[119]

Materials

Sticky notes

What It Is

Regular use of cognitive-neutralizing strategies is associated with good psychological health and with the use of problem-focused coping, so this exercise is designed to familiarize you with these strategies and help you to rehearse them and introduce them into your life on a regular basis.

How Will It Help My Worrying?

When you find the cognitive-neutralizing strategies that suit you and your particular worry at the time, these strategies can have added value. They will hopefully make you feel less anxious about your worry, and you will find it easier to become distracted from your worry. In addition, research has also shown that these strategies facilitate the transition to task-oriented coping.[120] That is, using these types of neutralizing strategies helps you find suitable solutions for your worries, and this will help you tackle worries in a genuine, cool-headed, problem-solving manner.

How to Do It

Five different types of cognitive-neutralizing strategies are listed below, each associated with a set of statements that you can apply to any individual worry that you want to downgrade. This is especially useful for worries over which you have little or no control or worries that are less important but keep preying on your mind. The five strategies are (1) downward comparison, (2) positive reappraisal, (3) cognitive disengagement, (4) optimism, and (5) life perspective.

Downward comparison is designed to devalue a threat by comparing your position or your worry with those of others who are much worse off than you. *Positive reappraisal* stresses the importance of focusing on what good might come out of your worry. *Cognitive disengagement* involves rehearsing statements that down-grade the importance of your worry. *Optimism* is a common positive attribute in which you can put the worry into perspective by considering ways in which it will turn out to be okay. Finally, *life perspective* enables you to consider your worry in relation to a wider lifelong perspective.

Cognitive-Neutralizing Strategies

Downward comparison:

"Other people are worse off than me."

"At least I still have my health and faculties."

"Things could be much worse than they are."

"It's not as bad as the things that happen to other people."

"Despite what's happening, I'm really lucky in other ways."

"Much worse things than this might have happened."

"People go through this sort of thing every day."

"A lot of people are in a worse position."

Positive reappraisal:

"This will make me a stronger person."

"I will come out of this experience better than I went in."

"In every problem, there is something good."

"I am capable and can overcome this."

Cognitive disengagement:

"The problems involved in this situation simply aren't important enough to get upset about."

"This situation isn't worth getting upset about."

"There's nothing more I can do, so I might as well stop worrying."

"Getting worked up about something won't solve it."

Optimism:

"Everything will work itself out in the end."

"I must just give it time to resolve itself."

"I'm sure everything will turn out alright in the end."

"Time solves most problems."

"This won't last forever."

Life perspective:

"My life will still continue whatever happens."

"Life goes on whatever happens."

"I can put up with these problems as long as everything else in my life is okay."

"At least I'm still alive."

"I might be feeling down at the moment, but this feeling is usually only temporary."

Consider each of the statements above in relation to worries you want to neutralize or downgrade the importance of. Once you've used these strategies, you may find that some of them suit you better than others, and those will be the ones to focus on in the future. Also, some strategies will be more appropriate for some worries than others (for example, life perspective strategies may be inappropriate for worries that have to do with health problems), so consider this when selecting which strategies to use.

It's important that you become familiar with these neutralizing statements and integrate them into your daily life as well as you can. Here are some ways to do this:

- Place one or two of the statements that you think are particularly relevant to your worries in prominent places around the house (for example, on the fridge or on a screensaver on your laptop).

- Share some or all these statements and discuss them with your family members, your significant other, or your best friend. The support of such people will help you practice what you preach and integrate these principles into your daily life.

- Get into the habit of using these principles whenever you can in your daily life. For example, when you're worried that a bad thing is likely to happen, try to think about that worry in the context of one or more of the neutralizing statements (for example, *I'm worried about what will happen to me after my divorce, but I know this will make me a stronger person*).

- Each day choose one statement or one type of neutralizing strategy and consider how that principle might influence how you do things and how you think about things on a daily basis (for example, *When I'm worried about something, I must remember that there are many people worse off than me*).

- Take some time to think about what your core goals are in life (for example, *to have a happy and content relationship with my partner* or *to have a successful career*) and think about how these principles might help you to achieve these goals.

TIP

Marlene found that she could use these neutralizing statements in a number of different ways to help her manage her worrying. She found that some statements were positive and reassuring in their own right, such as, "In every problem there is something good," and "This will make me a stronger person." She placed them in various places around the house so she would be reminded of them.

Other statements were helpful in relation to specific worries. For example, in relation to her worries about finances, she was able to downgrade these by using a downward comparison statement, such as, "Despite what's happening, I'm really lucky in other ways," and in the case of her worry about her relationship with her partner, she was able to rein in her catastrophizing by using optimism and life perspective: "Everything will work itself out in the end," and "Life goes on whatever happens."

What Have We Done So Far?

In this chapter, I described some tools to help you acquire a basic understanding of your worry: Asking questions such as, What do I worry about? Where do I worry about it? What are my worry fears? And are my worries solvable?

You began by keeping a worry diary designed to give you some insights into your worries and, most importantly, to give you some idea of how much of your worrying was unfounded. The next step gave you some practice at categorizing your worries: Are the things you worry about really important to you, and if so, are they solvable?

The last two exercises are intended to begin reducing the negative impact of worrying on your daily life—first, by condensing your worrying into a specified period in your day and then by providing you with some cognitive-coping strategies to help you minimize the negative impact of your worries.

Hopefully, these exercises have put you on the road to reining in some of your uncontrollable worrying.

CHAPTER 9

The "Smart" Worrier

Become a "Smart" Worrier and Learn How to Problem Solve

Roadmap of the chapter. Why are worriers so bad at solving problems? In this chapter, I'll look at some of the reasons why catastrophic worriers usually turn out to be very bad problem solvers and then describe what we can do to correct this state of affairs. Being a "smart" worrier requires a number of skills—practicing positive rather than negative thinking, being a realistic thinker who can differentiate solvable problems from imagined or hypothetical ones, and developing the ability to solve problems in a step-by-step way that leads to successful implementation of a solution. That's all in this chapter, together with a couple of exercises to help you identify what kind of thinker you are and how you can develop a systematic approach to problem solving.

When you stand back and take a big-picture look at what worrying is, it reveals itself as a complex conundrum full of contradictions. Worriers hold very strong beliefs that worry is an important thing to do; otherwise, bad things will happen. Yet they simultaneously hold the negative belief that when they worry, it will cause them distress and anxiety.

Similarly, most worriers will say that their worrying is a necessary attempt to deal with future events that they see as threatening or challenging. Yet they have poor confidence in their ability to solve these problems. So, worriers have poor problem-solving confidence. Yet when you force them to focus on finding a solution to a problem, they can come up with as good a solution as anybody.

Finally, worry is regularly defined as a problem-solving process—but catastrophic worriers regularly end up defining more problems and generating few solutions. These conundrums seem to be at the heart of pathological worrying and are created because the catastrophic worrier has real problems with problem solving, and this is what I'm going to address in this chapter.

The Worrier's Problem-Solving Problems

WORRY FACT 1. Chronic worriers adopt a "negative problem orientation" that can prevent positive problem solving and can generate dysfunctional ways of dealing with problems.

WORRY FACT 2. Catastrophic worriers often implement impulsive "quick fixes" for their problems to help alleviate distress, but these "quick fixes" may simply create further problems.

WORRY FACT 3. Worriers often adopt avoidant strategies in the hope that the problem will "go away" or indulge in repetitive rumination that generates more negative outcomes and no solutions.

I pointed out in chapter 1 that catastrophic worriers have poor problem-solving confidence. But the worrier's attitude about problem solving is more complicated than that. If you're a regular worrier, then you know that you often feel uncertain about how to deal with problems in life, and this lack of confidence often leads to worry. In chapter 1, I called this a form of "self-bashing" as themes of personal inadequacy, low self-esteem, and lack of control over events spill into the worry narrative. However, recent research suggests that chronic worriers are not just lacking confidence in their problem-solving ability, but they actually have negative attitudes toward problems—by that I mean attitudes that interfere with problem solving and prevent the implementation of practical solutions to their problems.

Negative problem orientation is defined as "a set of beliefs reflecting perceived threat of problems to well-being, doubt concerning problem-solving ability, and a tendency to be pessimistic about the outcome,"[121] and measures of negative problem orientation are highly correlated with measures of pathological worrying.[122] But these negative beliefs about problem solving don't just disrupt successful problem solving; they also appear to generate dysfunctional ways of dealing with problems.

Worriers avoid having to engage in a problem-solving process that they believe will be both unsuccessful and distressing by adopting alternative strategies aimed at summarily eliminating the problem or avoiding the problem that's causing the stress. These strategies include implementing impulsive quick fixes to help alleviate the distress caused by the worry as soon as possible, adopting an avoidant approach in the hope that the problem will simply "go away," or adopting an inflexible thinking style that keeps the worrier "stuck" in a ruminative process that leads to inaction. Let's look at these alternatives individually.

First, the "quick fix" strategy is a tendency to behave rashly and without forethought when experiencing stress or anxiety in an attempt to fix the problem quickly and reduce distress.[123] This is basically a "mood repair" approach that will rarely be properly thought out and in the long run is likely to create further problems. Its purpose is simply to make you feel better here and now. For example, when having an ongoing worrying argument about finances with your partner, a quick fix might involve trying to end the argument by criticizing your partner's capabilities or threatening to end the relationship—neither of which is likely to solve any issues about finances but may well create many further relationship problems. This results in failing to consider other solutions or the potential consequences of the quick fix and is implemented solely as an emotion-regulation strategy.

Second, the avoidant approach may involve waiting for the problem to be solved on its own or by shifting the responsibility to someone else. This strategy is often associated with interpersonal worries—especially if the worrier has difficulties dealing with interpersonal relationship problems[124]— and is often associated with an affiliative-submissive interpersonal style, which is when the worrier is often taken advantage of by significant others, such as their partner, and has difficulty asserting their needs.[125] This can result in the worrier simply passing responsibility for problems to the dominant other person or indulging in a range of avoidance activities that will prevent problem solving but partially alleviate the emotional distress caused by worries, such as spending money, excessive eating, or alcohol use—activities that prevent attempts to generate practical solutions to problems.

Third, the catastrophic worrier will often avoid practical problem solving by getting "stuck" in a repetitive, ruminative thinking process that generates more negative outcomes to the worry and no solutions. I've deliberately used the word "stuck" here because this process inevitably leads to inaction and maintains high levels of stress and anxiety—prolonged levels of distress that may eventually tip the worrier into rash actions that are instigated solely to relieve distress but may subsequently only make matters worse. Essentially, catastrophic worrying is not an attempt to solve the problem; rather, it provides a stubborn way of avoiding problem solving and leads the worrier to believe that they're simply not capable of dealing with their problems in a measured and practical way.

The upshot of all this is that chronic worriers don't just have poor confidence in their ability to solve problems; they actively indulge in strategies that prevent practical problem solving. So, this introduces us to the purpose of this chapter: to provide advice on becoming a "smart" worrier and learning to deal with worries in a positive problem-solving manner. Next, we'll discuss ways to develop positive and realistic thinking and then look at steps involved in active problem solving.

Be Positive, Be Realistic

WORRY FACT 4. Developing both positive thinking and realistic thinking are important ways of counteracting negative-thinking biases.

WORRY FACT 5. Being realistic is being objective about your problems and avoiding negative biases. Being positive is about approaching solutions to problems with confidence and skill.

Catastrophic worrying in and of itself doesn't solve anything. But it does signal that there's a problem that needs solving, so it's best to approach the problem positively and realistically. Positivity and realism are different things, so we'll deal with them separately. *Positivity* is important because of how anxiety becomes associated with a threat interpretation bias (as I described in chapter 6). That is, when confronted with ambiguous information, the anxious individual is likely to interpret it as negative rather than positive, and this negativity bias can become an ingrained characteristic of anxious worriers. *Realistic thinking* is also important when it comes to problem solving, and you need a clear mind that can differentiate facts that are real from those that are imagined or merely hypothetical. We'll begin this section with an exercise that will provide you with some insight into the kind of thinker that you are: positive or negative.

EXERCISE 14: What Kind of Thinker Are You?

I won't give too much away about this exercise before you complete it. I'll just say that it's designed to give you insight into the kind of thinker you are, and it will provide you with feedback that you can consider in the context of the remaining exercise in this chapter.

Materials

Pen or pencil

Notebook or Hypothetical Diary Entries worksheet (available for download at http://www.newharbinger.com/50348)

What It Is

This exercise includes a series of brief entries from a hypothetical diary. When you've completed the exercise, I'll explain the purpose of it and what your own pattern of responses indicates about your thinking.

How to Do It

Imagine the following are entries from your diary. Read each entry and then decide whether the event would cause you some concern (worry) or not. If you are using a notebook, be sure to write the relevant letter (A, B, or C) next to each entry—you'll use these for scoring later. If you think the event would cause you concern, check the box marked "concerned" on the worksheet or note that in your notebook. If you do not think it would cause you any undue concern, check the box marked "unconcerned" on the worksheet.

Please select only one response for all entries. There are no right or wrong answers to this; just decide how you would feel in each case. Complete your responses before you read the information below on how to score this exercise.

		Hypothetical Diary Entries		
	Date	Entry	Concerned	Unconcerned
B	Monday, May 23	I have so much work to do at the moment, and on top of all the essays that I have to write, we were told that we would be having a test next week too.		

	Date	Entry	Concerned	Unconcerned
A	Tuesday, May 24	My summer job applications are going well. So far, I have been offered second interviews by all three of the companies I'd most like to work for.		
C	Wednesday, May 25	I got an assignment back today and was surprised at the grade I received.		
C	Thursday, May 26	Mom had to take my little brother to the doctor today. The doctor was going to check his growth.		
B	Friday, May 27	I went to the hairdresser this morning, my new hairstyle is atrocious, and I look awful.		
C	Saturday, May 28	I got my first paycheck from my job today. When I got home, I was astonished to see how much was in it.		
A	Sunday, May 29	I went to Amanda's party last night; it was terrific.		
B	Monday, May 30	I have been feeling ill all day. If I still feel like this tomorrow, I will have to go to the doctor.		
A	Tuesday, May 31	It is a lovely day. I find it easy to be cheerful when the sun is shining.		
C	Wednesday, June 1	While on my way out tonight, I was stopped in the street.		
C	Thursday, June 2	The teams for the volleyball competition were announced today. I can't believe that I have been picked to play for the second team.		

	Date	Entry	Concerned	Unconcerned
A	Friday, June 3	I have just booked our summer vacation. I found a really good deal online for a two-week trip.		
C	Saturday, June 4	I was walking along the beach when I saw my friend, Helen, waving in the ocean.		
B	Sunday, June 5	We invited some friends over for a barbeque, but no one showed up.		
B	Monday, June 6	I received a letter from the bank this morning telling me that I have exceeded my overdraft limit and will have to pay quite heavy bank charges.		
C	Tuesday, June 7	I called the doctor today and was surprised to hear the results of last week's checkup.		
B	Wednesday, June 8	Not only was yesterday's meal out very disappointing, but I now also think that I have food poisoning.		
C	Thursday, June 9	My boss discussed the company's poor performance and agreed that I was the most responsible.		
C	Friday, June 10	On my first night as a chef in the restaurant, I was called to diners' tables twice.		
C	Saturday, June 11	At the reception, I stood up and made a speech, which made everybody laugh.		
A	Sunday, June 12	I really enjoyed seeing my old school friend, David, last night. It has been at least a year since we last got together.		

	Date	Entry	Concerned	Unconcerned
B	Monday, June 13	While I was at the water cooler, I overheard my workmates saying how much they disliked me.		
C	Tuesday, June 14	My performance in the play was commented on by everyone.		
A	Wednesday, June 15	A group of friends and I had planned a weekend away at the beginning of next month. Unfortunately, it has to be postponed for a couple of weeks, and I won't be able to go now as I am working.		
C	Thursday, June 16	On walking into the bank, I saw the bank teller handing over lots of money to a man.		
A	Friday, June 17	I was really pleased when I passed my driving test today. This calls for a big celebration.		
A	Saturday, June 18	I had a successful shopping trip this afternoon and bought a beautiful outfit to wear to my cousin's wedding.		
B	Sunday, June 19	As I walked along the lake, I slipped and twisted my ankle. It really hurts.		

Scoring

Add up the number of times you responded "concerned" for the "A" items, then do this separately for all "B" items, and then for all "C" items. Write down the total for each.

What does it mean?

- We asked a group of people to rate each item on how positive or negative it is. Items labeled A were considered to be "unambiguously positive," those labeled B were considered to be "unambiguously negative," and those labeled C were considered to be "ambiguous," or could be interpreted as either positive or negative.

- There are eight "A" items, eight "B" items, and twelve "C" items.

- Therefore, if you have a bias toward negative thinking, you probably circled more than half of the items (more than six) in the ambiguous category (category C) as causes for concern. The more items you checked beyond six in this category, the greater your negative interpretation bias.

- In addition, if you are a negative thinker, you may even have checked some of the items in category A (the unambiguously positive category) as causes for concern. We know that catastrophic worriers in particular note items in this category as causes for concern because they will often see negative features in events that many other people would see as overwhelmingly positive.

How Will This Help My Worrying?

If this exercise identified you as a possible negative thinker, don't panic! You are in the company of a significant percentage of the population—research conducted by the National Science Foundation estimates that around 80 percent of most people's daily thoughts are negative ones! But the more you noted items in category C as causes for concern, the greater your bias toward interpreting events and information as negative. Your glass will be half empty rather than half full, and it's a bias that will simply give you more and more things to worry about.

Next we're going to take a look at realistic thinking, and then I'll guide you through processes that will promote positive problem solving, but in the meantime, the "Tips" section provides some tips to help you manage negative interpretation biases and promote positive, optimistic thinking.

TIPS

If you want to be a positive thinker, you'll need to practice some concrete examples of positive thinking and positive behavior on a daily basis. Here are some examples to get you started.

- Start every day with a positive phrase such as, "Today is going to be a good day," or "Today I'm going to succeed in everything I do." Write the phrase on a sticky note and stick it on the bathroom mirror where you'll read it every morning.

- There's on old Dutch proverb that I'm very fond of: "If we don't learn from our mistakes, what's the point in making them?" Exactly. Nobody's perfect, so you'll have failures, and you will make mistakes, but turn these into lessons that offer positive advice for the future.

- Use humor to turn difficult situations into lighter ones. Humor will lift your mood if you feel low and banish negative thoughts from your mind. Seek out the company of humorous people and try laughing at life rather than fearing it.

- Most of our negative thoughts relate to things in the past or in the future. So why not focus on the present? Try focusing on this one particular moment that you're in right now, and the events that generated those negative thoughts won't seem so bad after all. You can try the mindfulness exercise in chapter 10 if you prefer a more structured approach to focusing on the present.

- Keep a "daily positivity diary." Each day, write down positive experiences, whether they're things that you've done, things you've seen other people do, or even just positive feelings you've had. Positive things happen to most people on a daily basis, but negative thinkers rarely recognize them or recall them at the end of the day. So, let's make these experiences explicit. Write them down, review them, and you will begin to absorb positivity into your life.

Even in the best of times, people are rarely objective observers of the world. We all develop thinking shortcuts that enable us to understand what's going on in the world quickly and efficiently. We use stereotypes to help us categorize things, and we regularly deploy heuristics as shortcuts to help us make rapid judgments about people and events (see examples of heuristics in chapter 1). But thinking shortcuts can often turn into whole-sale biases that distort our perception of the world and, as a consequence, warp our view of reality—and this is frequently what happens with anxious worriers. The anxious worrier ends up adopting thinking shortcuts that eventually become "thinking traps" because they only permit conceptions of the world as a dangerous, threatening place that the anxious worrier should be continuously wary of. Recovering from this state of chronic anxiety requires the worrier to identify negative thinking biases and to replace these with more realistic ways of thinking.

It was the father of cognitive behavior therapy, American psychiatrist Aaron T. Beck, who first identified many of the unrealistic thinking biases characteristic of anxious and depressed individuals, and some of these are listed in the table below. Take a look through the list to see if you can iden-tify any of these biases in your own thinking.

Unrealistic Thinking Biases		
Unrealistic Thinking Bias	**Description**	**Examples**
Jumping to conclusions	Jumping to a conclusion when evidence is lacking or is contrary to the conclusion	"Everyone hates me." "I will faint." "I'm going crazy."
Selective filtering	Abstracting a detail out of context and missing the significance of the whole situation	Believing that an audience hated your presentation because just a few people looked bored even though most people were attentive
Overgeneralization	Unjustified generalization on the basis of a single incident	Saying to yourself, "I never do anything right," on the basis of a single mistake
Black-and-white thinking	Events are labeled as black or white, good or bad, wonderful or horrible	Assuming everyone will either accept you or reject you
Personalization	Interpreting events in terms of their personal meaning to you rather than their objective characteristics	Believing that a frown on another person's face means they are annoyed specifically with you
Catastrophizing	Imagining the worst possible thing is about to happen even though it rarely does	"My partner hasn't come home on time. They must have had an accident."
Irrational beliefs	Setting extreme standards for yourself that you're unlikely to be able to achieve	"I must be loved by everyone." "I must never make mistakes."
Negative predictions	Always predicting that things will turn out badly	"I know I'll mess up."

Most of these biases generate negative ways of viewing the world or create guesses about what is happening that regularly turn out to be erroneous. They are all ways of thinking that will maintain your view of the world as a dangerous place that you should always be wary of.

Identifying these thinking biases in your own worrying is the first step to replacing these with more realistic thinking. When you start to worry, ask yourself questions that challenge any negative thinking biases, such as:

- Have I fallen into the trap of predicting that things will turn out badly before the event has occurred?

- Am I basing my judgments about this worry on the way I feel, rather than on the true facts?

- What's the worst thing that could happen? If it did happen, how would I cope with it?

While we're talking about reality, let's be honest. It's not going to be easy managing and changing ingrained negative thinking habits that you may have been nurturing over a lifetime, so be prepared to provide yourself with good practical support while you're trying to make these changes. For example, try to come up with statements about how you can cope, how your worries are not as bad as they may seem, and what a positive and resourceful person you yourself are. You can ask a partner or friend who knows you well to help you generate these statements. Then write them down on index cards or on your smartphone and carry them around with you, making sure you read them at least once a day. Coping statements might include things like, "When bad things have happened before, I've managed to handle them okay," or "I only need to do my best, whatever happens."

To downgrade some of your anxieties, you could use some of the cognitive-neutralizing statements provided in exercise 13 in chapter 8—statements like, "Time solves most problems," "Despite what's happening, I'm really lucky in other ways," or "This will make me a stronger person." Positive self-statements are all about being kind to yourself and include things like, "I can do it!" or "Everyone makes mistakes; if I make a mistake, I'm not a useless person."

Being realistic is being objective about your problems and avoiding negative biases. Being positive is about approaching solutions to problems with confidence and skill and, most importantly, ensures you learn from mistakes rather than simply taking them as evidence that you're a hopeless person. Everyone has to learn how to deal with life's problems, and it's never too late to start.

Have a Problem-Solving Session

Catastrophic worriers rarely solve problems because they tend to spend most of their time defining new ones. To break this cycle of problem-generation, it's best to adopt a systematic approach to solving problems—one that requires you to explicitly sit down, break the habit of ruminating solely about negative outcomes, and have a good, honest problem-solving session. This will focus your mind on the exact problem that's bothering you, help you define it in practical terms rather than in terms of how it makes you feel, force you to brainstorm some creative solutions, and most importantly, lead to you implementing those solutions. The steps to successful problem solving are outlined in the following exercise.

EXERCISE 15: Develop Your Problem-Solving Skills

If you're a catastrophic worrier, you'll spend most of your time defining worries rather than trying to solve them, so to break this negative cycle, it's best to develop a systematic, structured way of solving problems, and that is what this exercise offers. The exercise will guide you through all the specific steps required to begin generating practical solutions to your worries.

Materials

Pen or pencil

Notebook

Problem-Solving Worksheet (described below and available for download at http://www.newharbinger.com/50348)

What It Is

This exercise will guide you through all the necessary steps to begin defining some solutions to your worries and, most importantly, to implementing those solutions.

How Will This Help My Worrying?

As I've described earlier, catastrophic worriers tend to have a negative problem orientation. That is, they not only lack confidence in their problem-solving abilities, but they also adopt strategies that can interfere with problem-solving and prevent implementation of practical solutions to their problems. This exercise guides you through the individual steps required to solve a problem in an explicit way that you can use as a template for dealing with future worries.

How to Do It

Draw a Problem-Solving Worksheet as shown below or download a copy. This worksheet shows each stage of the problem-solving process, and I included examples using one of Marlene's worries from chapter 8.

The Problem-Solving Worksheet (with Marlene's examples)
Step 1. What is your worry?
What is the worry you would like to solve?
What if the car doesn't start and I'm late for work? It seems to happen often.
Step 2. What do you want to achieve?
What do you want to change or achieve? (Try to set a precise goal, not simply just feeling better.)
Regularly getting to work on time so my boss doesn't penalize me for being late.

Step 3. Brainstorming solutions

Try to think of several possible ways you might solve your worry.

1. Get the car serviced regularly.

2. Ask a neighbor who works near me to give me a ride to work.

3. Call in to work and let them know I'll be late when the car won't start.

4. Use public transportation instead of my car when the car doesn't start.

5. Call in sick on days when the car doesn't start.

Step 4. Evaluating potential solutions

List the positive and negative consequences of each of your potential solutions.

Positive	Negative
1. I'll be more confident the car will start. I'll get to work on time more often than I have in the past. I'll spend less money on getting repairs done if the car breaks down less often.	1. It will cost me money to get the car serviced regularly.
2. Some of my neighbors work near me and can drop me off at work. I could get to know my neighbors better.	2. They may not be going to work that day. They may not want to take a passenger. They may think I'm taking advantage of them. Their car may be broken down too. They may work different hours to me.
3. My boss will know I'm trying to get to work, but that I'll be late.	3. They may have to reschedule meetings. It might look like I'm lazy or unreliable coming in late.
4. It's an alternative way I can get to work that day.	4. I'll still be late if the car doesn't start. Public transportation in my area can be unreliable and unpunctual. I'll have to pay more to travel by public transportation.
5. If I say I'm sick, my boss will understand why I'm not at work.	5. I'll be a liar if I'm not really ill. I'll have to make sure no one sees me outside the house that day. If I call in sick too often, I may get disciplined at work.

Step 5. Selecting a solution

Choose your solution. Make a clear choice and set a time limit for achieving your goal (in step 2).

Get the car serviced regularly. Get it serviced in the next week and then regularly every six months.

Step 6. Planning the solution

What practical plans do you need to make to implement your solution? What resources do you need? What will you do, when, and who with?

1. Call the mechanic tomorrow morning.

2. Schedule the car for service as soon as possible.

3. Arrange alternative transportation to work on the day the car is being serviced.

4. Set an alert to remind me every six months to get the car serviced.

Step 7. Implementation

Do it! At this stage, don't worry about being successful, but write down any difficulties you might have had in implementing your solution.

Everything worked out as planned.

Step 8. How did it go?

If your solution worked, that's great! If it didn't, go back to step 4 and try another solution. Write down what you've learned from attempting this solution and use it as a learning exercise.

I learned how to sit down and generate solutions to problems and how to decide which solution to implement. I now feel much more confident that my car will start each morning. As a result, I hardly worry at all now about not getting to work on time.

Choose a worry that you'd like to solve. Before you choose your worry, it's best to fill in the Worry Categories Worksheet (exercise 11 in chapter 8). This will make it easier to identify a worry that's both important and can be solved (as opposed to worries that may not be so important or cannot be solved). One of Marlene's worries that fell into this category was *"What if the car doesn't start and I'm late for work?"*

Set a precise goal for your problem-solving efforts by defining what exactly you want to achieve. This should be a practical goal and not simply that you just want to feel better.

Try to think of as many possible ways as you can to possibly solve your problem and list them in the worksheet. Be creative and use your past experiences to help you to define possible solutions. The more you practice brainstorming like this, the easier it becomes to generate potential solutions.

Now think about the possible positive and negative consequences of each potential solution. List as many as you can for each solution. It's probably best to think of all the advantages before you think about disadvantages; otherwise, you may become unnecessarily disillusioned.

On the basis of your assessment of each solution in step 4, make a decision about which solution you want to attempt. Make a clear choice and set a practical time frame for implementing the solution.

Plan how you're going to implement the solution. Do this in detailed individual steps if you can, steps that will be easy to follow when the time comes to implement the plan. In this step, you will also need to consider what resources you'll need to implement the plan and whether you'll need the help of anyone else.

Do it! This is the step that most worriers find the most difficult. I described in chapter 1 that many worriers can often think up quite acceptable solutions to problems but lack the confidence to implement the solution. Don't worry about whether the solution will work or not; just try it out. If it doesn't work, you can always try another solution. You'll never find solutions to your problems unless you try them out.

Learn from your problem-solving experiences. Write down what you've learned from this particular experience—both things that worked well and things that didn't work quite so well. If your solution was effective, make sure you reward yourself—you deserve it!

Being a Smart Worrier

Worries are problems that need to be solved, yet those who worry most are arguably the ones who solve the least. To break the cycle of simply defining problem after problem without a solution, the catastrophic worrier has to acquire some new ways of thinking. In this chapter, we've covered three topics: moving away from negative thinking biases to more positive thinking; thinking realistically to differentiate real, solvable problems from imagined or hypothetical ones; and developing a step-by-step problem-solving strategy that is practical, explicit, and leads to the effective implementation of solutions. Master these skills and you're well on the way to becoming a "smart" worrier.

CHAPTER 10

Accentuate the Positive, Eliminate the Negative

*Tweaking Your Worry
to Make It Adaptive*

Roadmap of the chapter. Worrying is not all bad, and it does have some potentially good features to it. So this chapter is all about accentuating the positive and eliminating the negative—tweaking your worry to get the best out of it. The first part of the chapter discusses how you can tailor the exercises described in this book to manage some of the causes of catastrophic worrying. I'll also describe how psychological interventions, such as cognitive behavioral therapy (CBT), can be used to treat more severe cases of pathological worrying, such as generalized anxiety disorder (GAD). The latter half of this chapter focuses on some surprising upsides to worry and some of its more adaptive features—features that we can potentially harness to our advantage.

Targeting the Causes of Your Catastrophic Worrying

WORRY FACT 1. The causes of maladaptive worrying can be divided into distal causes that are largely in our past and proximal causes that influence our thinking each time we worry.

By and large, those of us who are worriers are not "born worriers." We're "contrived worriers" shaped by our experiences to view the world as challenging, threatening, and unpredictable. This leaves us with a personality that simply can't contemplate the future without detailed analysis, copious catastrophizing, and as a result, significant torment. And what do we do after having suffered all this torment and analysis? We procrastinate and agonize, and trap ourselves in a purgatory of inaction that leaves us to stew in our worrisome anxiety.

So, how can we target our worry to make it more adaptive? First, we need to look at the causes of our maladaptive worry, and these causes can be divided into two rather different levels of explanation. The fancy names for these different levels of explanation are "distal causes" and "proximal causes." Distal causes are experiences that are relatively remote from our worrying here and now, but over the years, have influenced the way we think about the world and ourselves. *Distal causes* are developmental factors that may have caused you to become a pathological worrier in the first place. We discussed many of these distal causes in chapter 2 when we covered childhood and adolescence developmental experiences and how these experiences shape the way we view the world.

Proximal causes refer to the cognitive and psychological factors that influence our thinking each time we worry. *Proximal causes* are the factors that affect persistence and distress during an individual worry bout. So proximal causes are the specific processes that make our individual worry bouts catastrophic, perseverative, distressing, and seemingly uncontrollable—factors I've discussed in the second part of this book. The lists below summarize the distal and proximal causes of catastrophic worrying that we've discussed so far.

Distal causes of pathological worrying:

- *Inconsistent or neglectful parenting* causes attachment anxiety, attachment avoidance, or intolerance of uncertainty.

- *Intrusive, harsh, or controlling parenting* results in poor ability to cope with negative events.

- *Maternal role reversal and enmeshment* results in the child's need to be continually prepared for threats and challenges.

- *Overprotective parenting* creates a vulnerability to anxiety and worry.

- *Experiencing negative life events* develops beliefs that the world is a dangerous and unpredictable place.

- *Brain function diversities* can limit ability to control and manage thoughts or regulate emotions.

- *A modest level of inherited characteristics* can influence anxiety levels and make worrying chronic.

Proximal causes of pathological worrying:

- *Poor problem-solving confidence* causes worrying to perseverate.

- *Negative mood* causes worrying to perseverate, increases performance standards, provides implicit information that worry goals have not been achieved, and triggers systematic processing of information.

- *Ingrained beliefs about worry being necessary to avoid bad things happening* generate longer worry bouts.

- *Intolerance of uncertainty* can make worry perseverative and distressing.

- *Anxiety* is associated with a series of cognitive biases that make worry unproductive and distressing:
  - attentional biases to threat
  - the interpretation of ambiguous information as threatening
  - the prevention of active problem solving.
- *Deployment of goal-directed worry stop rules during worrying* leads to longer worry bouts.

Research on the distal causes of worrying is still very patchy and under-developed—largely because long-term research is needed to understand these factors. It requires studies that map individuals' early developmental experiences and follow those individuals into adolescence and adulthood to discover how their early experiences are associated with subsequent tendencies to worry. That's the kind of research that needs considerable stamina, resilience, and large numbers of amenable participants—as well as significant amounts of funding.

In contrast, the study of proximal causes is relatively more straightforward. We can take individuals into the experimental psychology laboratory and—in highly controlled conditions—investigate how a variety of cognitive, psychological, and physiological factors influence their tendency to worry. From these individual experiments, we can then piece together proximal causes and begin to describe the psychological "mechanism" that generates a bout of catastrophic worrying—fitting together the pieces of the jigsaw to create a meaningful picture of how catastrophic worrying works each time we worry.

Matching Exercises to Causes

WORRY FACT 2. With every individual cause of pathological worrying we identify, we can develop ways of counteracting that specific cause.

The proximal causes of catastrophic worrying that we've identified so far are listed above. We've discovered many of the pieces of the jigsaw, but we're still a little way away from fitting them all together to create the big picture. But the good news is that with every individual causal factor we identify, we can develop ways of counteracting that cause of catastrophic worrying, and that's what's provided in many of the exercises in this book.

The table below lists the proximal causes of catastrophic worrying and identifies the exercises that might be used to ameliorate those causes and help you manage your catastrophic worrying. But don't just jump straight to the exercises; you'll get the most out of these exercises by rereading the chapters in which those exercises are introduced. That puts them into their relevant context along with how the causal factors work to generate your catastrophic worrying in the first place.

Exercises for Individual Worry Symptoms and Proximal Causes	
Worry Symptom / Proximal Cause	**Relevant Exercises**
Uncontrollable or perseverative worry	Exercise 12: Scheduling Daily Worry Time (chapter 8) Exercise 4: Managing Your News Consumption (chapter 3) Exercise 5: Managing Your Worry at Night (chapter 4)
Poor problem-solving confidence or inability to implement solutions to problems	Exercise 11: Managing Your Worries by Their Ability to Be Solved (Chapter 8) Exercise 15: Develop Your Problem-Solving Skills (chapter 9)
Negative mood and the associated increased performance standards, the implicit information that worry goals have not been achieved, and the systematic processing of information	Exercise 6: Boosting Your Mood (chapter 6) Exercise 8: Identify and Change Your Implicit Worry Rules (chapter 7)

Worry Symptom / Proximal Cause	Relevant Exercises
Ingrained beliefs about worry being necessary to avoid bad things happening	Exercise 12: Scheduling Daily Worry Time (chapter 8) Exercise 13: Downgrade Your Worries (chapter 8)
Intolerance of uncertainty	Exercise 9: Learning to Live with Uncertainty (chapter 7)
Anxiety and its associated cognitive biases: attentional biases to threat, the interpretation of ambiguous information as threatening, the prevention of active problem solving	Exercise 7: Ten Tips for Managing Your Anxiety (chapter 6) Exercise 15: Develop Your Problem-Solving Skills (chapter 9)
Deployment of goal-directed worry stop rules during worrying	Exercise 8: Identify and Change Your Implicit Worry Rules (chapter 7)

Cognitive Therapy for Pathological Worrying

WORRY FACT 3. For more severe forms of worrying, such as those found with a diagnosis of GAD, most treatment guidelines recommend face-to-face CBT.

WORRY FACT 4. Recovery rates for more severe forms of pathological worrying are between 57 and 60 percent regardless of whether treatment is by cognitive therapy or relevant medications.

All the exercises in this book are designed so you can attempt them on your own, and rereading individual chapters can help you identify the important proximal causes that either trigger or maintain your worrying. You can then attempt the relevant exercises that are designed to help manage these cognitive causes of your catastrophic or pathological worrying—and specifically, addressing these proximal causes is a primary aim of CBT for maladaptive worrying.[126]

However, for more severe forms of worrying—such as those associated with GAD—most guidelines recommend face-to-face CBT with an accredited therapist as the first-line treatment.[127] Face-to-face CBT therapy for pathological worrying normally involves exercises to address the client's intolerance of uncertainty (see chapter 7), sessions to help the client reevaluate their beliefs about the usefulness of worry (see chapter 5), and engaging the client in individualized behavioral experiments to help the client confront and manage persistent worries and fears.

But we need to be clear that GAD is more than just pathological worrying (see chapter 4). It's a condition that has other related symptoms, such as feeling continuously on edge, difficulty concentrating, irritability, muscle tension, and sleep disturbance. This combination of symptoms makes it a psychological condition that can sometimes be difficult to treat successfully. In particular, while CBT is more successful than many other forms of treatment for managing GAD symptoms, only just over half of those treated for GAD recover sufficiently to no longer be diagnosed with GAD.

In our research at the University of Sussex, my colleagues Fidelma Hanrahan, Andy Field, Fergal Jones, and I carried out a review of studies investigating the efficacy of cognitive therapies for GAD. We found that cognitive therapies were significantly more effective at dealing with the symptoms of GAD than nontherapy control conditions. But, very much to our surprise, the data suggested that only 57 percent of GAD participants were considered recovered twelve months after the end of their cognitive therapy treatment (in other words, only 57 percent were no longer diagnosable with GAD).[128] Sadly, this is far from unusual with any form of treatment for GAD.

First, is a recovery rate of 57 percent enough to justify fifty years of developing psychotherapeutic treatments for mental health disorders such as GAD? To be sure, GAD is a very stubborn condition. Long-term studies of GAD indicate that around 60 percent of people diagnosed with GAD still exhibit significant symptoms of the disorder twelve years later (regardless of whether or not they'd had treatments for these symptoms during this period).[129] If we apply this to the prevalence figures we normally see for

GAD, it means that the number of people in the US suffering long-term symptoms of GAD during their lifetime might be as high as fifteen million.

Second, what do we tell the pathological worrier with a diagnosis of GAD? Mental health problems, such as GAD, are distressing and disabling, and hope of recovery is the belief that most sufferers will take into treatment. Let's take the optimistic view and assume that 57 percent of those treated with cognitive therapy will fully recover. This level of hope is not just reserved for cognitive therapy for GAD or psychotherapies in general. It's a figure that pretty much covers pharmaceutical treatments for GAD as well, with remission and recovery rates for drug treatments being around 60 percent.[130]

But as I've frequently advocated in this book, catastrophic worrying is not a biological given; it's a learned activity. So, if it's learned, it can surely be unlearned, and we're very much in the process of developing more effective treatments for pathological worrying generally and GAD in particular. Recent interventions designed by Colette Hirsch and colleagues at the Institute of Psychiatry in London aim to target cognitive biases that maintain catastrophic worrying, and her studies have impressive results.

These interventions target implicit cognitive biases, such as negative-interpretation biases and attention biases to threat (see chapter 6), and repair an impaired ability to redirect attention away from worry. Initial studies indicate that post-treatment recovery was indicated for three out of every four clients with GAD—a significant improvement on recovery rates reported for earlier forms of cognitive therapy.[131]

The message is that there's a lot going on to try to understand why many of us are pathological and catastrophic worriers, and as we grow our understanding of these distressing activities, we're actively putting that knowledge to good use and developing many different ways to help the worrier manage their worrying.

This is all good news, so let me end this book on a similar positive note. Does worrying have any upsides? Yes, some psychologists believe it does.

Worrying as a Positive Practice in Everyday Life

WORRY FACT 5. Worrying has some surprising upsides, including acting as a motivator and an emotional buffer.

WORRY FACT 6. Worrying can have some adaptive consequences, such as protecting against accidental death and motivating the individual to take health-related preventative and protective precautions.

All worriers have good reasons why they worry—regardless of whether or not their worry causes them distress. Some want to actively solve problems; others will say they just want to be prepared to face upcoming challenges. On some level, everyone agrees that worrying is a good and necessary thing to do.

Is it a good and necessary thing to do? Well, I regularly get emails from business coaches and corporate management trainers asking me how they can harness their employees' anxious worrying in more positive ways. They see the analytical energy that goes into worrying and wonder how this might be channeled into the strategic and operational tasks required in the workplace. To be sure, if you're an entrepreneur planning to promote your new startup, worry can be a powerful motivator for success and can influence your thinking to help you come up with practical strategies to grow your business. Worry is a forward-thinking process, but it needs to be linked to decisions, solutions, and actions if it's to be truly helpful. Let's look at this more closely.

First, much of the worrying I've discussed in this book is primarily maladaptive. It involves generating negative outcomes rather than solutions, and in many cases, it's associated with extreme distress and anxiety. Can any good be found in this form of worrying?

Kate Sweeny and Michael Dooley at the University of California at Riverside believe that worrying has some "surprising upsides."[132] They point out that some studies suggest that people who worry a lot are more likely to perform well in the workplace and in law school and seek information in response to stressful events. But they single out two other constructive aspects of worry as being of particular importance: worry as a motivator and worry as an emotional buffer.

First, worry may be important in productive planning for important future events and as a predictor of being at risk for undesirable future outcomes. These factors are especially important in motivating preventative-health behaviors, and studies have demonstrated that high worriers are more likely to use seatbelts, indulge in safe sex practices, get vaccinated, and undergo cancer screening. Effectively, anxious catastrophic worrying may facilitate the generation of numerous negative health outcomes that motivate the individual to take preventative and protective precautions.

So, does anxious worry really bestow the protective effects that these studies suggest, or is it all in vain? Well, yes, it does seem to endow some adaptive advantages. William Lee, a psychiatrist at London's Institute of Psychiatry, looked at the lives of 5,362 people born in 1946. He discovered that those who exhibited high levels of worrisome anxiety (based on ratings by their teachers when they were thirteen years old) were significantly less likely to die an accidental death than those with low anxiety.[133] Only 0.1 percent of the anxious individuals died accidentally compared with 0.72 percent of the nonanxious individuals. There was no difference between the two groups on the number of nonaccidental deaths. But there does appear to be a cost to this.

After twenty-five years of age, the worrisome individuals started to exhibit higher mortality rates due to illness-related deaths than their non-anxious counterparts. Lee and his colleagues concluded that their results "suggest there are survival benefits of increased trait anxiety in early adult life, but these may be balanced by corresponding survival deficits in later life associated with medical problems"—this latter outcome represents the abrasive effect of worry on physical health that we discussed in detail in chapter 4.

Second, Sweeny and Dooley argue that worrying can act as an emotional buffer. It does this by serving as a "low-water mark" by which other emotional states seem pleasurable in contrast. They argue that if people's worrying over a future outcome is sufficiently intense and unpleasant, their emotional response to the actual outcome will seem less unpleasurable in comparison to their previous worried state. This is known as "bracing for the worst" and consists of embracing a pessimistic outlook in anticipation of the arrival of uncertain news in an effort to mitigate disappointment if the news is bad and augment elation and excitement if the news is good.[134] This may in part explain why many people worry about future events that are effectively uncontrollable, such as an impending exam result, the health of a close relative, or the effects of international conflicts. People tend to feel better about bad things that happen if they feared for the worst rather than assumed the best.

So there do appear to be some positives in a catastrophic worry process that generates primarily negative outcomes. But can we harness the systematic processing generated by our worry to create positive outcomes?

Tweaking Your Worry to Make It Useful

WORRY FACT 7. Catastrophic worrying can act as a potentially useful risk-assessment tool.

WORRY FACT 8. Catastrophic worrying can be "slowed down" by replacing negative "What if...?" questions with more positive "So then what...?" questions.

The big problem with catastrophic worrying is that it rarely generates solutions, only more potential bad outcomes. Even when it does generate a solution, the cognitive biases that fuel that worry process immediately lead the worrier to finding would-be flaws and hidden traps within those solutions. This process helps explain why the catastrophic worrier rarely implements any of the solutions that they might occasionally come up with—why try a solution if you think it might be flawed? That's a process that chips away at your problem-solving confidence, and that's not something that helps when it comes to moving forward in life.

How can we tweak our catastrophic worrying to make it genuinely useful? Well, without any tweaking at all, our catastrophic worrying makes us aware of risks when we're dealing with a problem. So even as is, it's a potentially useful risk-assessment tool that'll help you catalog many of the possible bad outcomes that a problem may encompass. As we discussed earlier, you can use this process constructively if you're trying to make a decision that requires some form of risk assessment—for example, decisions about your health, your safety, or some aspect of your life that may involve potential costs or penalties.

But your worry usually lists only the negatives. You'll still need to come up with some potential solutions to help you deal with the risks you've identified. For example, if your worrying has identified potential health risks, there may be medical solutions that'll mitigate the risks, such as getting vaccinated to lower the risk of contracting specific diseases and illnesses. Don't forget, where potentially important risks and costs are involved, avoidance is not a good coping option because you're leaving yourself open to the possible negative consequences you've identified. It's smart to consider solutions that'll reduce the risks you've identified, so let's look at some ways of introducing solution-generation into your worrisome thinking.

The generation of bad outcomes that comes with catastrophic worrying can be overwhelming, so we need to slow it down a bit. This can be done by replacing "What if...?" questions with "So then what...?" questions that focus on how you'd deal with any particular hypothetical outcome. If you're worried that one of your customers won't pay their bill at the end of the month, the "So then what...?" line of self-questioning can often both diffuse the distress generated by your catastrophic worrying and suggest solutions. For example, "If they don't pay their bill, I'll still be able to cover my costs for the next month. So then what...? I can look at ways of seeking payment from the customer next month. So then what...? If I can get them to pay a portion of their bill over the next three months, that would be okay." That's a much healthier process than if we'd posed negativity-laden "What if…?" questions at each step.

Once we've slowed the catastrophizing process down a bit by introducing "So then what…?" questions, we will be better placed to transition from negativity-laden worry to problem solving. There are three questions to ask in relation to each hypothetical bad outcome: (1) How plausible is this outcome? (Is it very likely to happen?) (2) Is it something I have control over? (If I come up with a solution, is it something I could implement successfully?) (3) Can I do something about this problem now? (What can I do right now to begin to solve the problem?)

If the worry is something you don't have control over or can't do anything about right now, there's little point to continuing with catastrophic or perseverative worrying, so you'll want to disengage from the worry process. Exercise 6 in chapter 6 can help to distract you from your worry and boost your mood, and exercise 13 in chapter 8 provides some tips on how to downgrade your worries using cognitive-neutralizing strategies.

But there are other simple strategies that can help—including exercising, postponing your worry by writing it down with the intention of coming back to it later, or simply engaging with positive images. For example, researchers at the Institute of Psychiatry in London have shown that asking worriers to generate vivid images of situations in their lives that have turned out positively (even ones unrelated to their current worry) significantly reduced negative worry intrusions and reduced anxiety.[135] Because worry is primarily a verbal activity, generating positive images not only interferes with this activity but also creates positive vibes that reduce anxiety. Why don't you generate a few scenarios from your own life where things have worked out positively for you and refer to these when trying to disengage from your worrying? Create mental images for these scenarios and keep them in mind. This will help prevent you from engaging in the verbal activity that is the basis of most of our worrying.

Finally, if your "What if…?" catastrophizing has generated a negative outcome that is something you have control over and you can do something about now, then it's time for some problem solving. If you're unsure how to approach a problem-solving task, then you can try exercise 15 in chapter 9. This exercise provides a step-by-step structure to problem solving and information on how to find suitable, implementable solutions for your worries. It's a process that can not only supply you with a plan A, but it can also generate a plan B, and even a plan C if plan A becomes impractical.

The "Surprising Upsides" of Worrying

Catastrophic worrying can be used as a risk-assessment process that generates potential negative outcomes—especially when making decisions about aspects of your life that may involve potential costs or penalties.

Worry can act as a motivator to take protective or preventative actions when it comes to making decisions about your health and safety.

Anxious worriers are less likely than nonworriers to die an accidental death in the first half of their lives—possibly as a result of their ability to identify and avoid potential threats and challenges in life.

People who worry a lot are more likely to perform well in the workplace and in law school and seek information in response to stressful events.

Worrying can act as an emotional buffer because people tend to feel better about bad things that happen if their worrying made them fear the worst rather than assume the best.

So, worrying does have its upsides, but it still needs a little management to generate the benefits it has to offer. I can't emphasize enough that when left alone to do its thing, catastrophic worrying is an uncontrolled force, commandeering most of our thoughts, generating hypothetical negative scenarios, and causing distress and even disability in those most affected. But if you're up to it, a few tweaks here and there, which I've described above, can slow its negativity and introduce some time for problem-solving thought—an end product that is arguably the true purpose of the act of worrying.

The Future of Worrying

Worrying will be with us for as long as we experience threats and challenges in our lives—so don't expect it to disappear from the face of the earth anytime soon. And indeed, it may even be on the increase in many spheres of modern society.[136] Worry has been around since organisms developed the higher-cognitive capabilities that allow them to remember the past, experience the present, and plan for the future, so it isn't just you that worries, so too does your dog, your cat, and probably even the birds in your garden and the mice in your cupboard.

Worry evolved to help organisms identify future threats and then plan how to avoid them. But for us poor human beings, this process regularly goes dramatically wrong and creates psychological distress and stymies productivity. However, as we've seen in this chapter, even if worrying becomes catastrophic, perseverative, distressing, and seemingly uncontrollable, it still bestows some adaptive advantages. So we need to understand how to maintain those adaptive advantages without suffering the psychological distress that comes with extreme and negative forms of worrying. Because worrying is potentially such a useful psychological process, the exercises in this book are not solely about preventing your worrying but are designed to help you to streamline your worrying as a problem-solving process that you can deploy when required to help you negotiate life's more challenging scenarios.

Finally, most of our worrying tends to be about the future, so make sure your worrying is productive and distress-free because the future is where you're going to spend the rest of your life. But right now, you're in the present, so enjoy that too, which is why I'm ending this book with one final exercise: a mindfulness meditation exercise to help you relax. May you appreciate the present, fondly anticipate the future, and no longer be a slave to catastrophic worrying.

EXERCISE 16: Mindfulness Meditation to Help You Relax

Try this mindful breathing exercise to help you relax when you feel stressed.

Materials

Your mind

Your body

A quiet space

What It Is

This exercise is designed to help you relax and focus on the present. It's a type of meditation in which you focus on what you're sensing and feeling in the present moment, and you do this without interpretation of those feelings or making judgments about what those feelings mean. It uses guided imagery and breathing exercises to relax your body and mind and reduce stress.

How Will This Help My Worrying?

You can use this exercise whenever you feel stressed or anxious, and you can also use it immediately after you've attempted one of the other worry exercises in this book or after your daily worry time (exercise 12).

How to Do It

Close your eyes, place a hand on your stomach, and focus on your stomach as it rises and falls. Don't try to force your breath; just accept it as is.

Imagine your breath going down your body into both legs and feet. What does this contact feel like?

Try to picture your breath rising up your body from your feet and legs.

Focus your breathing and awareness on your stomach area and become aware of any sensations.

Now, become aware of your breathing around the areas of your chest and upper back.

Next, guide your breathing gently down each arm to your fingertips and then back up to your shoulders. Observe any feelings you have in your shoulders, arms, wrists, and hands as you go.

Finally, focus your awareness on the neck and up into your head, becoming aware of any facial expressions and any tense feelings in your neck and head.

As you continue focusing on your breathing, feel kindness toward yourself for relaxing your body in this way and then gently and slowly open your eyes.

Endnotes

Chapter 1

1   K. Quindlen, "How to Tell If Your Mind Suffers from 'Catastrophizing,'" The Everygirl, October 28, 2018, https://theeverygirl.com/catastrophizing/.

2   G. Davey, *The Anxiety Epidemic: The Causes of Our Modern-Day Anxieties* (London, UK: Constable & Robinson, 2018).

3   G. C. L. Davey and S. Levy, "Catastrophic Worrying: Personal Inadequacy and a Perseverative Iterative Style as Features of the Catastrophizing Process," *Journal of Abnormal Psychology* 107 (1998): 576–586.

4   G. C. L. Davey, "The Catastrophizing Interview Procedure," in *Worry and Its Psychological Disorders: Theory, Assessment, and Treatment*, eds. G. C. L. Davey and A. Wells (New York: John Wiley & Sons, 2008).

5   H. M. Startup and G. C. L. Davey, "Mood as Input and Catastrophic Worrying," *Journal of Abnormal Psychology* 110 (2001): 83–96.

6   M. Vasey and T. D. Borkovec, "A Catastrophizing Assessment of Worrisome Thoughts," *Cognitive Therapy and Research* 16 (1992): 505–520.

7   T. Gilovich, D. Griffin, and D. Kahneman, *Heuristics and Biases: The Psychology of Intuitive Judgment* (Cambridge, UK: Cambridge University Press, 2002).

8   G. C. L. Davey, "Worrying, Social Problem-Solving Abilities, and Social Problem-Solving Confidence," *Behaviour Research & Therapy* 32 (1994): 327–330.

9   G. C. L. Davey, M. Jubb, and C. Cameron, "Catastrophic Worrying as a Function of Changes in Problem-Solving Confidence," *Cognitive Therapy & Research* 20 (1996): 333–344.

10   PR Moment, "UK Tops the Charts for Negative News Stories," June 25, 2019, https://www.prmoment.com/pr-research/uk-tops-the-charts-for-negative-news-stories.

11   W. M. Johnston and G. C. L. Davey, "The Psychological Impact of Negative TV News Bulletins," *British Journal of Psychology* 88 (1997): 85–91.

12   G. C. L. Davey, "A Mood-as-Input Account of Perseverative Worrying," in *Worry and Its Psychological Disorders: Theory, Assessment, and Treatment*, eds. G. C. L. Davey and A. Wells (New York: John Wiley & Sons, 2006).

13   R. J. Melton, "The Role of Positive Affect in Syllogism Performance," *Personality and Social Psychology Bulletin* 21 (1995): 788–794.

14   S. R. Dash, F. Meeten, and G. C. L. Davey, "Systematic Information Processing Style and Perseverative Worrying," *Clinical Psychology Review* 33 (2013): 1041–1056.

15   F. Meeten and G. C. L. Davey, "Mood-as-Input Hypothesis and Perseverative Psychopathologies," *Clinical Psychology Review* 31 (2011): 1259–1275.

Chapter 2

16   K. L. Purves, J. R. I. Coleman, S. M. Meier, C. Rayner, K. A. S. Davis, R. Cheeseman, et al., "A Major Role for Common Genetic Variation in Anxiety Disorders," *Molecular Psychiatry* 25 (2019): 3292–3303; M. G. Gottschalk and K. Domschke, "Genetics of Generalized Anxiety Disorder and Related Traits," *Dialogues in Clinical Neuroscience* 19 (2017): 159–168.

17   S. M. Meier, K. Trontti, K. L. Purves, T. Damm, J. Grove, M. Laine, et al., "Genetic Variants Associated with Anxiety and Stress-Related Disorders: A Genome-Wide Association Study and Mouse-Model Study," *JAMA Psychiatry* 76 (2019): 924–932.

18   J. Bowlby, *Attachment and Loss, Vol. 2, Separation: Anxiety and Anger,* International Psycho-Analytical Library, no. 95 (London, UK: Hogarth Press, 1973).

19   A. L. Sanchez, P. C. Kendall, and J. S. Comer, "Evaluating the Intergenerational Link Between Maternal and Child Intolerance of Uncertainty: A Preliminary Cross-Sectional Examination," *Cognitive Therapy and Research* 40, no. 4 (2016): 532–539.

20   F. Meeten, S. R. Dash, A. L. S. Scarlet, and G. C. L. Davey, "Investigating the Effect of Intolerance of Uncertainty on Catastrophic Worrying and Mood," *Behaviour Research and Therapy* 50, no. 11 (2012): 690–698.

21   C. J. Wright, G. I. Clark, A. J. Rock, and W. L. Coventry, "Intolerance of Uncertainty Mediates the Relationship Between Adult Attachment and Worry," *Personality & Individual Differences* 112 (2017): 97–102.

22   A. M. Brown and S. P. Whiteside, "Relations Among Perceived Parental Rearing Behaviors, Attachment Style, and Worry in Anxious Children," *Journal of Anxiety Disorders* 22 (2008): 263–272.

23   L. Shanahan, W. Copeland, E. J. Costello, and A. Angold, "Specificity of Putative Psychosocial Risk Factors for Psychiatric Disorders in Children and Adolescents," *Journal of Child Psychology & Psychiatry* 49 (2008): 34–42.

24   S. A. Wijsbroek, W. W. Hale, Q. A. Raaijmakers, and W. H. Meeus, "The Direction of Effects Between Perceived Parental Behavioral Control and Psychological Control and Adolescents' Self-Reported GAD and SAD Symptoms," *European Child & Adolescent Psychiatry* 20 (2011): 361–371.

25   J. Cassidy, J. Lichtenstein-Phelps, N. J. Sibrava, C. L. Thomas, and T. D. Borkovec, "Generalized Anxiety Disorder: Connections with Self-Reported Attachment," *Behavior Therapy* 40 (2009): 23–38.

26   Tribune Media Wire, "Helicopter Parenting: Dad Uses Drone to Walk Daughter to School," April 22, 2015, http://whnt.com/2015/04/22/ helicopter-parenting-dad-uses-drone-to-walk-daughter-to-school/.

27   J. L. Hudson and R. M. Rapee, "Parent-Child Interactions in Clinically Anxious Children and Their Siblings," *Journal of Clinical Child & Adolescent Psychology* 31 (2002): 548–555.

28   G. S. Ginsburg and M. C. Schlossberg, "Family-Based Treatment of Childhood Anxiety Disorders," *International Review of Psychiatry* 14 (2002): 143–154.

29   J. R. Cougle, K. R. Timpano, H. Sachs-Ericsson, M. E. Keough, and C. J. Riccardi, "Examining the Unique Relationships Between Anxiety Disorders and Childhood Physical and Sexual Abuse in the National Comorbidity Survey-Replication," *Psychiatry Research* 177 (2010): 150–155.

30 A. Moulton-Perkins, A. Whittington, and M. Chinery, "Working with People with Anxiety Disorders," in *Clinical Psychology*, eds. G. Davey, N. Lake, and A. Whittington (New York: Routledge, 2015).

31 E. Paulesu, E. Sambugaro, T. Torti, L. Danelli, F. Ferri, G. Scialfa, et al., "Neural Correlates of Worry in Generalized Anxiety Disorder and in Normal Controls: A Functional MRI Study," *Psychological Medicine* 40, no. 1 (2010): 117–124.

32 A. Etkin, K. Prater, F. Hoeft, V. Menon, and A. Schatzberg, "Failure of Anterior Cingulate Activation and Connectivity with the Amygdala During Implicit Regulation of Emotional Processing in Generalized Anxiety Disorder," *American Journal of Psychiatry* 167, no. 5 (2010): 545–554.

33 J. Mohlman, R. B. Price, D. A. Eldreth, D. Chazin, D. M. Glover, et al., "The Relation of Worry to Prefrontal Cortex Volume in Older Adults with and Without Generalized Anxiety Disorder," *Psychiatry Research* 173 (2009): 121–127.

34 Flourishing Families Clinic, https://www.flourishingfamiliesclinic.nhs.uk.

35 C. Creswell and L. Willetts, *Helping Your Child with Fears and Worries* (London, UK: Robinson, 2019).

Chapter 3

36 T. A. Brown, M. M. Antony, and D. H. Barlow, "Psychometric Properties of the Penn State Worry Questionnaire in a Clinical Anxiety Sample," *Behaviour Research and Therapy* 30 (1992): 33–37.

37 R. Pintner and J. Lev, "Worries of School Children," *The Journal of Genetic Psychology* 56 (1940): 67–76.

38 P. A. Wisocki, B. Handen, and C. Morse, "The Worry Scale as a Measure of Anxiety Among Homebound and Community Active Elderly," *Behavior Therapist* 9, no. 5 (1986): 91–95.

39 F. Tallis, G. C. L. Davey, and A. Bond, "The Worry Domains Questionnaire," in *Worrying: Perspectives on Theory, Assessment, and Treatment*, eds. G. C. L. Davey and F. Tallis (New York: Wiley, 1994).

40 M. Craske, R. Rapee, L. Jackel, and D. Barlow, "Qualitative Dimensions of Worry in DSM III-R Generalized Anxiety Disorder Subjects and Nonanxious Controls," *Behaviour Research & Therapy* 27 (1989): 397–402.

41 A. Reeves, D. Stuckler, M. McKee, D. Gunnell, S.-S. Chang, and S. Basu, "Increase in State Suicide Rates in the USA During Economic Recession," *Lancet* 380 (2012): 1813–1814.

42 The World Bank, "COVID-19 to Add as Many as 150 Million Extreme Poor by 2021," https://www.worldbank.org/en/news/press-release/2020/10/07/covid-19-to-add-as-many-as-150-million-extreme-poor-by-2021.

43 M. Roser and E. Ortiz-Opsina, "Income Inequality," December 2013, https://ourworldindata.org/income-inequality.

44 M. Paskov, K. Gërxhani, and H. G. van de Werfhorst, "Income Inequality and Status-Seeking," INET Oxford Working Paper no. 2015-03, Institute for New Economic Thinking at the Oxford Martin School.

45 The US Burden of Disease Collaborators, "The State of US Health, 1990–2016," *JAMA* 319, no. 14 (2018): 1444–1572.

46 R. A. Cree, C. A. Okoro, M. M. Zack, and E. Carbone, "Frequent Mental Distress Among Adults, by Disability Status, Disability Type, and Selected Characteristics–United States 2018," *Centers for Disease Control & Prevention, Morbidity & Mortality Weekly Report* 69, no. 36 (2020): 1238–1243.

47 Craske et al., "Qualitative Dimensions of Worry in DSM III-R Generalized Anxiety Disorder Subjects and Nonanxious Controls."

48 Tallis et al., "The Worry Domains Questionnaire."

49 M. Morgan, "Sleepless Nights, Being Stuck in Traffic and Running Out of Loo Roll While on the Toilet: The Top 10 Everyday Things That Brits Find Most Stressful Revealed," Daily Mail, April 10, 2015, http://www.dailymail.co.uk/femail/article-3030649/Top-10-everyday-things-stress-Brits-revealed.html.

50 Sarah Cox, "'Fearcasting' to Blame for the Stress of Everyday Emergencies," Goldsmiths University of London, April 8, 2015, http://www.gold.ac.uk/news/fearcasting---i2-media-direct-line-study/.

51 J. A. Muñiz-Velázquez, D. Gómez-Baya, and J. L. Delmar, "Exploratory Study of the Relationship Between Happiness and the Rise of Media Consumption During COVID-19 Confinement," *Frontiers in Psychology* 12 (2021), https://doi.org/10.3389/fpsyg.2021.566517.

52 A. Ayala, O. Barzilay, and M. Perchick, "The Impact of Facebook on Social Comparison and Happiness: Evidence from a Natural Experiment," *SSRN* (February 13, 2017), https://doi.org/10.2139/ssrn.2916158.

53 J. Campisi, P. Bynog, H. McGehee, J. C. Oakland, S. Quirk, C. Taga, and M. Taylor, "Facebook, Stress, and Incidence of Upper Respiratory Infection in Undergraduate College Students," *Cyberpsychology, Behavior, and Social Networking* 15 (2012): 675–681.

54 J. K. Morin-Major, M.-F. Marin, N. Durand, N. Wan, R.-P. Juster, and S. J. Lupien, "Facebook Behaviors Associated with Diurnal Cortisol in Adolescents: Is Befriending Stressful?" *Psychoneuroendocrinology* 63 (2016): 238–246.

55 S. Allan, "Witnessing in Crisis: Photo-Reportage of Terror Attacks in Boston and London," *Media, War & Conflict* 7, no. 2 (2014).

56 D. Altheide, *Media Edge: Media Logic and Social Reality* (New York: Peter Lang, 2014).

57 J. Butler, *Notes Toward a Performative Theory of Assembly* (Cambridge, MA: Harvard University Press, 2015).

58 American Psychological Association, "APA *Stress in America Survey*: US at 'Lowest Point We Can Remember;' Future of Nation Most Commonly Reported Source of Stress," November 1, 2017, https://www.apa.org/news/press/releases/2017/11/lowest-point.

59 Davey, *The Anxiety Epidemic.*

60 Johnston and Davey, "The Psychological Impact of Negative TV News Bulletins."

Chapter 4

61 B. Verkuil, J. F. Brosschot, W. A. Gebhardt, and J. F. Thayer, "When Worries Make You Sick: A Review of Perseverative Cognition, the Default Stress Response and Somatic Health," *Journal of Experimental Psychopathology* 1 (2010): 87–118.

62   Brown et al., "Psychometric Properties of the Penn State Worry Questionnaire in a Clinical Anxiety Disorders Sample."

63   G. C. L. Davey, F. Eldridge, J. Drost, and B. A. MacDonald, "What Ends a Worry Bout? An Analysis of Changes in Mood and Stop Rule Use Across the Catastrophic Worry Interview," *Behaviour Research & Therapy* 45 (2007): 1231–1243.

64   E. A. Holman, R. Cohen Silver, M. Poulin, J. Andersen, V. Gil-Rivas, and D. N. McIntosh, "Terrorism, Acute Stress, and Cardiovascular Health," *Archives of General Psychiatry* 65 (2008): 73–80.

65   American Psychiatric Association, *Diagnostic and Statistical Manual of Mental Disorders, Fifth Edition, DSM-5* (Washington, DC: American Psychiatric Association, 2013).

66   A. M. Ruscio, L. S. Hallion, C. C. W. Lim, S. Aguilar-Gaxiola, A. Al-Hamzawi, J. Alonso, et al., "Cross-Sectional Comparison of the Epidemiology of DSM-5 Generalized Anxiety Disorder Across the Globe," *JAMA Psychiatry* 74 (2017): 465–475.

67   H. Haller, H. Cramer, R. Lauche, F. Gass, and G. J. Dobos, "The Prevalence and Burden of Subthreshold Generalized Anxiety Disorder: A Systematic Review," *BMC Psychiatry* 14 (2014): 128.

68   C. Thielsch, T. Ehring, S. Nestler, J. Wolters, I. Kopei, F. Rist, and T. Andor, "Metacognitions, Worry, and Sleep in Everyday Life: Studying Bidirectional Pathways Using Ecological Momentary Assessment in GAD Patients," *Journal of Anxiety Disorders* 33 (2015): 53–61.

69   W. R. Pigeon, T. M. Bishop, and K. M. Krueger, "Insomnia as a Precipitating Factor in New Onset Mental Illness: A Systematic Review of Recent Findings," *Current Psychiatry Reports* 19, no. 4 (2017), https://doi.org/10.1007/s11920-017-0802-x.

70   A. G. Harvey, A. L. Sharpley, M. J. Ree, K. Stinson, and D. M. Clark, "An Open Trial of Cognitive Therapy for Chronic Insomnia," *Behaviour Research & Therapy* 45 (2007): 2491–2501; A. G. Harvey, L. Bélanger, L. Talbot, P. Eidelman, S. Beaulieu-Bonneau, E. Fortier-Brochu et al., "Comparative Efficacy of Behavior Therapy, Cognitive Therapy, and Cognitive Behavior Therapy for Chronic Insomnia: A Randomized Controlled Trial," *Journal of Consulting & Clinical Psychology* 82 (2014) : 670–683.

71   M. Perego, V. A. Tyurin, Y. Y. Tyurina, J. Yellets, T. Nacarelli, C. Lin et al., "Reactivation of Dormant Tumor Cells by Modified Lipids Derived from Stress-Activated Neutrophils," *Science Translational Medicine* 12 (2020), https://doi.org/10.1126/scitranslmed.abb5817.

72   A. D. Kanner, J. C. Coyne, C. Schaefer, and R. S. Lazarus, "Comparison of the Two Modes of Stress Management: Daily Hassles and Uplifts Versus Major Life Events," *Journal of Behavioral Medicine* 4, no. 139 (1981).

73   A. A. Stone, B. R. Reed, and J. M. Neale, "Changes in Daily Event Frequency Precede Episodes of Physical Symptoms," *Journal of Human Stress* 13 (1987): 70–74.

74   M. Russell and G. C. L. Davey, "The Relationship Between Life Event Measures and Anxiety and Its Cognitive Correlates," *Personality & Individual Differences* 14 (1993): 317–322.

75   M. A. Rosenkranz, D. C. Jackson, K. M. Dalton, I. Dolski, C. D. Ryff, B. H. Singer, D. Muller, N. H. Kalin, and R. J. Davidson, "Affective Style and *In Vivo* Immune Response: Neurobehavioral Mechanisms," *PNAS* 16 (2003): 11148–11152.

76   Verkuil, Brosschot, Gebhardt, and Thayer, "When Worries Make You Sick."

77   L. D. Kubzansky, I. Kawachi, A. Spiro, III, S. T. Weiss, P. S. Vokonas, and D. Sparrow, "Is Worrying Bad for Your Heart?: A Prospective Study of Worry and Coronary Heart Disease in the Normative Aging Study," *Circulation* 95 (1997): 818–824.

78   J. F. Brosschot, B. Verkuil, and J. F. Thayer, "Exposed to Events That Never Happen: Generalized Unsafety, the Default Stress Response, and Prolonged Autonomic Activity," *Neuroscience & Biobehavioral Reviews* 74 (2017): 287–296.

79   C. Ottaviani, J. F. Thayer, B. Verkuil, A. Lonigro, B. Medea, A. Couyoumdjian, and J. F. Brosschot, "Physiological Concomitants of Perseverative Cognition: A Systematic Review and Meta-Analysis," *Psychological Bulletin* 142 (2015): 231–259.

Chapter 5

80   D. J. Goeway, "85 Percent of What We Worry About Never Happens," HuffPost, August 25, 2015, https://www.huffpost.com/entry/85-of-what-we-worry-about_b_8028368

81   L. S. LaFreniere and M. G. Newman, "Exposing Worry's Deceit: Percentage of Untrue Worries in Generalized Anxiety Disorder Treatment," *Behavior Therapy* 51 (2020): 413–423.

82   L. H. Corbit, J. L. Muir, and B. W. Balleine, "The Role of Nucleus Accumbens in Instrumental Conditioning: Evidence of a Functional Dissociation Between Accumbens Core and Shell," *Journal of Neuroscience* 21 (2001): 3251–3260.

83   G. C. L. Davey, F. Tallis, and N. Capuzzo, "Beliefs About the Consequences of Worrying," *Cognitive Therapy & Research* 20 (1996): 499–520.

84   F. Meeten, G. C. L. Davey, E. Makovac, D. R. Watson, S. N. Garfinkel, H. D. Critchley, and C. Ottaviani, "Goal-Directed Worry Rules Are Associated with Distinct Patterns of Amygdala Functional Connectivity and Vagal Modulation During Perseverative Cognition," *Frontiers in Human Neuroscience* 10, no. 553 (2016), https://doi.org/10.3389/fnhum.2016.00553.

85   N. J. Sibrava and T. D. Borkovec, "The Cognitive Avoidance Theory of Worry," in *Worry and Its Psychological Disorders*, eds. G. C. L Davey and A. Wells (New York: Wiley, 2006).

86   M. G. Newman and S. J. Llera, "A Novel Theory of Experiential Avoidance in Generalized Anxiety Disorder: A Review and Synthesis of Research Supporting a Contrast Avoidance Model of Worry," *Clinical Psychology Review* 31 (2011): 371–382.

87   G. C. L. Davey, F. Tallis, and N. Capuzzo, "Beliefs About the Consequences of Worrying," *Cognitive Therapy & Research* 20 (1996): 499–520

Chapter 6

88   P. A. Russell, "Fear-Evoking Stimuli," in *Fear in Animals and Man*, ed. W. Sluckin (New York: Van Nostrand Reinhold, 1979).

89   A. J. Ouimet, B. Gawronski, and D. J. A. Dozois, "Cognitive Vulnerability to Anxiety: A Review and Integrative Model," *Clinical Psychology Review* 29 (2009): 459–470.

90 C. MacLeod and I. L. Cohen, "Anxiety and the Interpretation of Ambiguity: A Text Comprehension Study," *Journal of Abnormal Psychology* 102 (1993): 238–247.

91 K. Mogg and B. P. Bradley, "A Cognitive-Motivational Analysis of Anxiety," *Behaviour Research and Therapy* 36 (1998): 809–848.

92 I. M. Engelhard and A. Arntz, "The Fallacy of Ex-Consequentia Reasoning and the Persistence of PTSD," *Journal of Behavior Therapy & Experimental Psychiatry* 36 (2005): 35–42.

93 G. C. L. Davey, J. Hampton, J. Farrell, and S. Davidson, "Some Characteristics of Worrying: Evidence for Worrying and Anxiety as Separate Constructs," *Personality & Individual Differences* 13 (1992): 133–147.

94 G. C. L. Davey, "Pathological Worrying as Exacerbated Problem-Solving," in *Worrying: Perspectives on Theory, Assessment, and Treatment,* eds. G. C. L. Davey and F. Tallis (New York: Wiley, 1994).

95 F. Tallis, M. Eysenck, and A. Mathews, "Elevated Evidence Requirements and Worry," *Personality and Individual Differences* 12 (1991): 21–27.

96 Davey, *The Anxiety Epidemic.*

97 Y. L. Ferguson and K. M. Sheldon, "Trying to Be Happier Really Can Work: Two Experimental Studies," *Journal of Positive Psychology* 8 (2012): 23–33.

98 M. Abreau, "Neuroscientists Calculates Feel-Good Top 10 Playlist," *Boston Globe,* September 25, 2015, https://www.bostonglobe.com/arts/2015/09/25/neuroscientist-calculates-feel-good-top-playlist/5SjZ0X8WvrztSiQDp1DGfP/story.html.

99 G. A. Panza, B. A. Taylor, P. D. Thompson, C. M. White, and L. S. Pescatello, "Physical Activity Intensity and Subjective Well-Being in Healthy Adults," *Journal of Health Psychology* (2017), https://doi.org/10.1177/1359105317691589.

100 A. McDermott, "The 18 Best Essential Oils for Anxiety," HealthLine, June 1, 2021, https://www.healthline.com/health/anxiety/essential-oils-for-anxiety#essential-oils-for-anxiety.

101 D. Donelli, M. Antonelli, C. Bellinazzi, G. F. Gensini, and F. Firenzuoli, "Effects of Lavender on Anxiety: A Systematic Review and Meta-Analysis," Phytomedicine 65 (2019), https://doi.org/10.1016/j.phymed.2019.153099.

102 T. W. Shin, M. Wilson, and T. W. Wilson, "Are Hot Tubs Safe for People with Treated Hypertension?" *Canadian Medical Association Journal* 169 (2003): 1265–1268.

103 Davey, *The Anxiety Epidemic.*

104 From Davey, *The Anxiety Epidemic,* chapter 12.

Chapter 7

105 G. C. L. Davey, H. M. Startup, C. B. MacDonald, D. Jenkins, and K Patterson, "The Use of 'as Many as Can' Versus 'Feel Like Continuing' Stop Rules During Worrying," *Cognitive Therapy & Research* 29 (2005): 155–169.

106 Startup and Davey, "Mood as Input and Catastrophic Worrying."

107 J. P. Forgas and R. East, "On Being Happy and Gullible: Mood Effects on Skepticism and the Detection of Deception," *Journal of Experimental Social Psychology* 44 (2008): 1362–1367.

108 Dash, Meeten, and Davey, "Systematic Information Processing Style and Perseverative Worry."

109 W. D. Scott and D. Cervone, "The Impact of Negative Affect on Performance Standards: Evidence for an Affect-as-Information Mechanism," *Cognitive Therapy & Research* 26 (2002): 19–37.

110 P. Pratt, F. Tallis, and M. Eysenck, "Information-Processing, Storage Characteristics, and Worry," *Behaviour Research and Therapy* 35, no. 11 (1997): 1015–1023.

111 G. C. L. Davey and F. Meeten, "The Perseverative Worry Bout: A Review of Cognitive, Affective, and Motivational Factors That Contribute to Worry Perseveration," *Biological Psychology* 121 (2016): 233–243.

112 J. F. Boswell, J. Thompson-Hollands, T. J. Farchione, and D. H. Barlow, "Intolerance of Uncertainty: A Common Factor in the Treatment of Emotional Disorders," *Journal of Clinical Psychology* 69 (2013), https://doi.org/10.1002/jclp.21965.

113 Julie Beck, "How Uncertainty Fuels Anxiety," *The Atlantic*, March 18, 2015, https://www.theatlantic.com/health/archive/2015/03/how-uncertainty-fuels-anxiety/388066/.

114 R. Jenkinson, E. Milne, and A. Thompson, "The Relationship Between Intolerance of Uncertainty and Anxiety in Autism: A Systematic Literature Review and Meta-Analysis," *Autism* 24 (2020): 1933–1944.

115 R. A. Vasa, N. L. Kreiser, A. Keefer, V. Singh, and S. H. Mostofsky, "Relationships Between Autism Spectrum Disorder and Intolerance of Uncertainty," *Autism Research* 11 (2018): 636–644.

116 C. Joyce, E. Honey, S. R. Leekam, S. L. Barrett, and J. Rodgers, "Anxiety, Intolerance of Uncertainty, and Restricted and Repetitive Behaviour: Insights Directly from Young People with ASD," *Journal of Autism Developmental Disorders* 47, no. 12 (2017): 3789–3802.

117 R. N. Carleton, M. K. Mulvogue, M. A. Thibodeau, R. E. McCabe, M. M. Antony, and G. J. Asmundson, "Increasingly Certain About Uncertainty: Intolerance of Uncertainty Across Anxiety and Depression," *Journal of Anxiety Disorders* 26, no. 3 (2012): 468–479.

Chapter 8

118 LaFreniere and Newman, "Exposing Worry's Deceit."

119 G. C. L. Davey and A. S. McDonald, "Cognitive Neutralising Strategies and Their Use Across Differing Stressor Types," *Anxiety, Stress & Coping* 13 (2000): 115–141.

120 G. C. L. Davey, "A Comparison of Three Cognitive Appraisal Strategies: The Role of Threat Devaluation in Problem-Focussed Coping," *Personality & Individual Differences* 14 (1993): 535–546.

Chapter 9

121 M. Robichaud and M. J. Dugas, "Negative Problem Orientation (Part 1): Psychometric Properties of a New Measure," *Behaviour Research and Therapy* 43, no. 3 (2005): 391–401.

122 M. J. Dugas, M. H. Freeston, and R. Ladouceur, "Intolerance of Uncertainty and Problem Orientation in Worry," *Cognitive Therapy and Research* 21 (1997): 593–606.

123 B. L. Malivoire, K. E. Stewart, K. Tallon, M. Ovanessian, E. J. Pawluk, and N. Koerner, "Negative Urgency and Generalized Anxiety Disorder Symptom Severity: The Role of Self-Reported Cognitive Processes," *Journal of Personality and Individual Differences* 145 (2019): 58–63.

124 B. L. Malivoire and N. Koerner, "Interpersonal Dysfunction in Individuals High in Chronic Worry: Relations with Interpersonal Problem-Solving," *Behavioural & Cognitive Psychotherapy* 50, no. 2 (2021), https://doi.org/10.1017/S1352465821000436.

125 T. M. Erickson, M. G. Newman, E. C. Siebert, J. A. Carlile, G. M. Scarsella, and J. L. Abelson, "Does Worrying Mean Caring Too Much? Interpersonal Prototypicality of Dimensional Worry Controlling for Social Anxiety and Depressive Symptoms," *Behavior Therapy* 47 (2016): 14–28.

Chapter 10

126 C. R. Hirsch, S. Beale, N. Grey, and S. Liness, "Approaching Cognitive Behavior Therapy for Generalized Anxiety Disorder from a Cognitive Process Perspective," *Frontiers in Psychiatry* 4 (2019), https://doi:.org/10.3389/fpsyt.2019.00796.

127 National Collaborating Centre for Mental Health, *Generalised Anxiety Disorder in Adults: Management in Primary, Secondary and Community Care*, NICE (Leicester, UK: British Psychology Society, 2011), https://www.ncbi.nlm.nih.gov/books/NBK83459/.

128 F. Hanrahan, A. P. Field, F. W. Jones, and G. C. L. Davey, "A Meta-Analysis of Cognitive Therapy for Worry in Generalized Anxiety Disorder," *Clinical Psychology Review* 33, no. 1 (2013): 120–132.

129 P. Tyrer, H. Sievewright, and T. Johnson, "The Nottingham Study of Neurotic Disorder: Predictors of 12-Year Outcome of Dysthymic, Panic, and Generalized Anxiety Disorder," *Psychological Medicine* 34 (2004): 1385–1394.

130 D. S. Baldwin, "Efficacy of Drug Treatments for Generalized Anxiety Disorder: A Systematic Review and Meta-Analysis," *British Medical Journal* 342 (2011): d1199.

131 Hirsch et al., "Approaching Cognitive Behavior Therapy for Generalized Anxiety Disorder from a Cognitive Process Perspective."

132 K. Sweeny and M. D. Dooley, "The Surprising Upsides of Worry," *Social and Personality Psychology Compass* 11, no. 4 (2017): e12311.

133 W. E. Lee, M. E. J. Wadsworth, and M. Hotopf, "The Protective Role of Trait Anxiety: A Longitudinal Cohort Study," *Psychological Medicine* 36 (2006): 345–351.

134 K. Sweeny, P. J. Carroll, and J. A. Shepperd, "Thinking About the Future: Is Optimism Always Best?" *Current Directions in Psychological Science* 15 (2006): 302–306.

135 C. Eagleson, S. Hayes, A. Mathews, G. Perman, and C. R. Hirsch, "The Power of Positive Thinking: Pathological Worry Is Reduced by Thought Replacement in Generalized Anxiety Disorder," *Behaviour Research & Therapy* 78 (2016): 13–18.

136 G. C. L. Davey, F. Meeten, and A. P. Field, "What's Worrying Our Students? Increasing Worry Levels Over Two Decades and a New Measure of Student Worry Frequency and Domains," *Cognitive Therapy & Research* (2021): 1–4, https://doi.org/10.1007/s10608-021-10270-0.

Graham Davey, PhD, is emeritus professor of psychology at the University of Sussex, UK; where his research interests are anxiety, worry, phobias, and the role of the disgust emotion in psychopathology. He has written a range of teaching and research books, most recently on clinical psychology and psychopathology. He is also past president of the British Psychological Society, and a founding editor in chief of the *Journal of Experimental Psychopathology*. He lives in Brighton, UK.

Real change *is* possible

For more than forty-five years, New Harbinger has published proven-effective self-help books and pioneering workbooks to help readers of all ages and backgrounds improve mental health and well-being, and achieve lasting personal growth. In addition, our spirituality books offer profound guidance for deepening awareness and cultivating healing, self-discovery, and fulfillment.

Founded by psychologist Matthew McKay and Patrick Fanning, New Harbinger is proud to be an independent, employee-owned company. Our books reflect our core values of integrity, innovation, commitment, sustainability, compassion, and trust. Written by leaders in the field and recommended by therapists worldwide, New Harbinger books are practical, accessible, and provide real tools for real change.

newharbingerpublications

MORE BOOKS from
NEW HARBINGER PUBLICATIONS

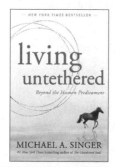

Did you know there are **free tools** you can download for this book?

Free tools are things like **worksheets, guided meditation exercises**, and **more** that will help you get the most out of your book.

You can download free tools for this book—whether you bought or borrowed it, in any format, from any source—from the New Harbinger website. All you need is a NewHarbinger.com account. Just use the URL provided in this book to view the free tools that are available for it. Then, click on the "download" button for the free tool you want, and follow the prompts that appear to log in to your NewHarbinger.com account and download the material.

You can also save the free tools for this book to your **Free Tools Library** so you can access them again anytime, just by logging in to your account! Just look for this button on the book's free tools page.

+ Save this to my free tools library

If you need help accessing or downloading free tools, visit **newharbinger.com/faq** or contact us at **customerservice@newharbinger.com**.